Exploring the Rain Forest

Multiple Intelligences & Cooperative Learning Activities

Laura Candler

Kagan

Kagan

©1999 by *Kagan Publishing*
This book is published by *Kagan Publishing*. All rights are reserved by *Kagan Publishing*. No part of this publication may be reproduced or transmitted in any form by any means, electronic or mechanical, including photocopy, recording, or any information storage and retrieval system, without prior written permission from *Kagan Publishing*. The blackline masters included in this book are intended for duplication only by classroom teachers who purchase the book, for use limited to their own classrooms. To obtain additional copies of this book, or information regarding professional development in cooperative learning or multiple intelligences, contact:

Kagan Publishing
981 Calle Amanecer
San Clemente, CA 92673
1(800) 933-2667
www.KaganOnline.com

ISBN: 978-1-879097-47-6

Table of Contents

Acknowledgments i
About the Author ii

Chapter 1

Introduction iv
The Eight Intelligences At-A-Glance ix
Chart of Activities & Curriculum Areas x
Chart of Activities & Multiple Intelligences xii
Chart of Structures & Activities xiv
Exploring the Rain Forest Pre/Post Test xv

Chapter 2

Rain Forest Activities 1

1. We Wonder 3
2. Action Letters 7
3. Tropical Products 13
4. Sentence Practice 17
5. Jungle Mapping 19
6. Word Power 25
7. Who Knows? 29
8. Rain Forest Factoids 31
9. Layers of Life 35
10. Comparing Climates 45
11. Dictionary Word Sort 53
12. Tropical Treasure Hunt ... 57
13. Medical Mysteries 63
14. Tropical Poetry 71
15. Rain Forest in a Bag 77
16. Vivid Vocabulary 81
17. It's About Time 89
18. Same-Different 93
19. Jigsaw Story Mapping 97
20. Comparing Kids 101
21. Erosion Experiment 205
22. Words in a Word 109
23. Traveling Showdown 111
24. Amazing Animals 115
25. Mystery Animal 121
26. Food Chain Fun 123
27. Create a Creature 129
28. Write Around 133
29. Math Talk 139
30. Causes and Effects 143
31. The Rain Forest Dilemma .. 147
32. Agreement Circles 151
33. Save the Rain Forest 153
34. Tropical Tunes 155
35. Puppet Shows 159
36. Concept Mapping 163

Table of Contents (continued)

Chapter 3
Cooperative Learning Structures 167

1. Agreement Circles 169
2. Blackboard Share 169
3. Find Someone Who 170
4. Jigsaw 170
5. Mix-Freeze-Group 171
6. Mix-Freeze-Pair 171
7. Numbered Heads Together .. 172
8. Pairs Compare 172
9. Pair Discussion 173
10. Pair Project 173
11. RallyRobin 174
12. RallyTable 174
13. RoundRobin 175
14. RoundTable 175
15. Same-Different 176
16. Showdown 176
17. Spend-A-Buck 177
18. Stand-N-Share 177
19. Team Discussion 178
21. Team Interview 178
22. Teammates Consult 179
23. Team Project 179
24. Think-Pair-Share 180

Chapter 4
Answers 181

4. Rain Forest Sentences for Practice 182
9. Rain Forest Layers Quick Quiz 183
23. Rain Forest Word Problems (Level A) 184
23. Rain Forest Word Problems (Level B) 185
29. Rain Forest Word Problems . 186

Chapter 5
Resources 187

Books 188
Music 189
Organizations 190
Internet Links 192

Exploring the Rain Forest by Laura Candler • **Kagan Publishing** • 1 (800) 933-2667 • www.KaganOnline.com

Acknowledgments

I would like to thank the many people who contributed their ideas, time, and expertise to this creation of this book. During the writing stage, a number of teachers at my school offered suggestions for the lessons and helped field-test the activities. In this regard, I appreciate the help of Jennifer Graham, Sandra Leechford, Jonnie Miller, and Susan Simon.

I would like to thank the folks at *Ranger Rick* magazine for granting permission to reprint the article, "In Search of Jungle Secrets." I am also grateful to Dr. Mark Plotkin, the subject of the article, for allowing a photograph of his work in the Amazon to be reprinted along with article itself.

Finally, I want to thank the members of the Kagan team for months of hard work and dedication during the production stage. I especially want to thank Miguel Kagan who was responsible for the book's overall design concept. In addition, Miguel was instrumental in managing the myriad details involved in the publication of *Exploring the Rain Forest*. I also appreciate the extensive work of graphic designer Karen Mannino who also designed portions of the book, created many illustrations and borders and for hand-coloring the cover illustration. Thanks to Celso Rodriguez for creating the cover illustration which brings the book to life. Together this team transformed my plain manuscript into an eye-catching and dynamic book!

About the Author

Laura Candler is a classroom teacher with 17 years experience in elementary and middle school education. She recently received national certification through the National Board for Professional Teaching Standards in the area of Middle Childhood education. She is currently teaching 4th grade at E. E. Miller Elementary School in Fayetteville, North Carolina. You may visit her class online by pointing your browser to Candler Kids on the Web **(http://home.att.net/~candlers)**.

Laura has used Kagan methods extensively for many years. She enjoys sharing these techniques through writing books and teaching educational workshops. She has trained hundreds of teachers in cooperative techniques, both within her school system and throughout the East Coast. Laura is the author of five other books for teachers: *Discovering Decimals, Science Buddies, Cooperative Learning and Hands-on Science, Cooperative Learning and Wee Science,* and *The Science Club Companion.*

Laura welcomes feedback concerning the lessons and activities found in her books. If you have a question or comment, feel free to contact her by e-mail at **candlers@att.net.**

Introduction

Why study the rain forest?

Despite the fact that many of us will never see tropical rain forests, we experience their impact on a daily basis. Rain forests cover less than 7% of the earth's surface, yet they are rightly called the "lungs of the earth." The dense vegetation provides oxygen to the entire planet. The tropics fuel our global weather system with rising currents of warm moist air. In addition, many of the products that we enjoy in the United States, from pineapples to wicker chairs, were discovered or originally produced in the rain forest. Millions of species of plants and animals make their home in the rain forest, many of which may provide humankind with medical cures or important scientific insights.

You might never visit a real rain forest, but you *can* explore the tropics from within your classroom. Tropical rain forests hold a fascination for children that is almost unmatched. Children seem to have an unlimited capacity for reading about the rain forest, watching videos of the amazing animals and plants, writing stories, and solving rain forest math problems.

Teaching students to be concerned about our earth is a curriculum objective at almost every grade level. By studying the rain forest, students learn that plants, animals, and people must all share this planet and its resources. We cannot destroy rain forests out of selfish disregard . . . because in so doing we will destroy ourselves.

Why use an integrated thematic approach?

Life is not arbitrarily divided into chunks — this is math, this is science, this is reading. Outside of the school environment, we approach new learning by integrating our past knowledge and a variety of skills. When we become interested in a topic, we read about it, analyze data, solve problems, discuss its impact on society, and perhaps even write letters expressing our views. When we are extremely interested in a new topic (say, learning about Brazil in preparation for a vacation to that country), we become totally immersed in the learning process. Our discoveries in one area fuel our interest in other related topics.

Why not tap into this natural approach to learning as we teach students in the classroom? Instead of reading a story about rain forests and then solving math word problems involving a trip to the supermarket, why not use one theme as a focus for all studies? Why not integrate the curriculum so that a discovery in one content area sparks a question to be investigated in another?

Tropical rain forests provide a wealth of opportunity for this type of integration. The science connections are obvious — studying the interaction of plants and animals, the oxygen cycle, human's impact on the environment, and so on. What may not be as obvious is the multitude of other curriculum areas that can be tied in.

The outpouring of information on this topic in recent years has been phenomenal. Type the words "rain forest" into any Internet search engine and you'll find a tremendous amount up-to-date information at your fingertips. Most major rain forest conservation organizations have created Web sites that are both entertaining and informative. Furthermore, by visiting those sites you can find links to other rain forest information on the web. A great place to start is the Rainforest Action Network (see the Rain Forest Resources starting on page 187).

In addition, a visit to the local bookstore reveals dozens of other print and nonprint resources on rain forest topics. You'll find wonderful children's fiction and nonfiction books, both read alouds and read alones. To help you find just the right book, an annotated bibliography of children's literature is located within the Rain Forest Resources (page 187). Many of the lessons in this book have a "literature link" suggested, but often you can substitute another book if the one listed is not available.

In addition to science and literature, your rain forest exploration can easily extend into math, health, social studies, language arts, and the arts. Studying about medical mysteries of the rain forest, solving word problems, writing stories, examining cultural differences, and creating puppet shows are examples of the many exciting activities that await your class.

Why cooperative learning?

If you are already using cooperative learning, you know that cooperative learning is a powerful teaching technique that students happen to love. Over 600 formal research studies have demonstrated benefits that run the gamut from improved academic achievement to better social skills and attitudes toward school. Being a part of a learning team is infinitely more exciting than a solitary excursion into academia. And when the classroom is an exciting place to be, students are motivated to work hard and accept increasingly difficult educational challenges. In addition, students in cooperative classrooms develop an appreciation for other learning styles and ways of thinking.

Imagine visiting two classrooms anywhere in the United States. Both are studying the rain forest. Step into the first classroom . . . shhh! Students seated in rows are reading an article entitled "What Are Rain Forests?" Immediately after they finish reading the teacher assigns five questions to answer in preparation for the class discussion. Students are absorbed in academic pursuits, but the lesson is hardly designed to instill a love of learning.

Step into the next classroom and the difference is immediately apparent. Students in teams of four are assigned a specific rain forest layer, such as the Canopy or Forest Floor. Each team member moves to a different corner of the room to meet with others who will become "experts" on that topic. The experts read about their topic and discuss the major concepts together. Each person draws a diagram of their rain forest layer to help them teach what they have learned. They return to their original teams and assemble their drawings into a layered diagram of the rain forest. As they work, they discuss what they learned about each layer. Through cooperative learning, studying the rain forest becomes an experience students will long remember.

Fortunately, you don't have to spend hours planning awesome cooperative lessons . . . this book is your key to success! In this book, you will find three dozen exciting activities designed to make your rain forest unit an unforgettable adventure.

What are structures?

The key to successful cooperative learning is proper implementation. And the best way to implement cooperative learning is to use cooperative learning strategies, or structures. Structures are step-by-step methods used to ensure that cooperative learning doesn't dissolve into groupwork. If activities are not properly structured, one person may end up doing all the work while the rest of the team enjoys a free ride. Well-structured cooperative activities require some type of individual accountability either through a written response, assigned roles, color-coding, or performance in front of a group. By using structures to build activities, all students are required to fully participate in each and every activity.

Structures have names such as Think-Pair-Share, Jigsaw, RoundTable, and Round-Robin. The activities in this book rely on structures, but you don't need to know the structure names to be successful with the activities. The activity directions are straightforward and assume no prior knowledge of specific cooperative techniques.

A brief structure reference is given in the appendix to this book. If you would like more detailed and comprehensive structure descriptions, read Dr. Spencer Kagan's book, *Cooperative Learning*. This is the ultimate handbook to implementing the structural approach. The book is available through **Kagan,** **1(800) 933-2667.**

Why multiple intelligences?

People are beginning to recognize something that teachers have instinctively known for many years: intelligence is not one-dimensional. Dr. Howard Gardner pioneered this body of research in 1983 with the release of his book, *Frames of Mind: The Theory of Multiple Intelligences*. The two basic ideas central to his theory are: 1) Intelligence is not fixed; we have the ability to develop intellectual capacity, and 2) There are many ways to be smart. There are at least eight different kinds of intelligence, ranging from Logical/Mathematical ability to Interpersonal intelligence. For a description of each of the eight intelligences, refer to the Eight Intelligences At-A-Glance chart (page ix).

As a long-time proponent of cooperative learning, Spencer Kagan immediately recognized the significance of Howard Gardner's theory. When implemented properly, cooperative learning techniques naturally incorporate many different intelligences. In fact, it would be almost impossible to utilize MI theory effectively *without* cooperative learning. Dr. Kagan and his son Miguel applied MI theory to cooperative learning practice and created a comprehensive handbook for teachers entitled *Multiple Intelligences: The Complete MI Book*. Within this book, they challenge educators to accept three visions with regards to implementing MI theory.

Vision 1: Matching. Teachers can enhance learning by *matching* instructional strategies with how students learn best. Traditional academic settings primarily rely on Logical/Mathematical and Verbal/Linguistic teaching strategies. Students who learn best in other ways will benefit from multiple approaches to instruction.

Vision 2: Stretching. The new view of intelligence offers hope for improving all of our intellectual capabilities. By using a wide variety of instructional approaches, teachers can *stretch* students to develop a full spectrum of abilities.

Vision 3: Celebrating. Since people are smart in many ways, teachers can encourage students to recognize and *celebrate* each other's uniqueness. As they consider their own abilities, students stop wondering "Am I smart?" and begin to ask themselves "What are the ways I'm smart?" This kind of validation does much to boost self-esteem and promote a positive, supportive classroom.

In order to meet the goals of Matching and Stretching, you will want to know which of the eight intelligences are utilized during each activity. Because of the nature of cooperative learning, all of the activities found in this book provide opportunities to develop Interpersonal intelligence. The remaining intelligences are represented throughout the book. Refer to the Chart of Activities & Multiple Intelligences (page xii) for specific activities and intelligences.

What about assessment?

Cooperative learning is a wonderful instructional technique, but it was never designed to be used 100% of the school day. Cooperative learning is primarily for practice and higher-level thinking. Cooperative activities should never be given group grades that feed into individual grades. Students still take tests individually. A Rain Forest Pre/Post Test has been provided for individual assessment.

Even though cooperative activities aren't used as formal assessment, you can use them to informally assess your students' knowledge of critical concepts. As students work in teams, move throughout the classroom listening to their conversations. You may hear misconceptions voiced that would never have been brought up in a class discussion. Remember to balance cooperative activities with individual assignments. It's easy to become so excited about cooperative learning that you forget the importance of individual work. If students become too dependent on their team, they may panic when given a job to do alone.

Having students write individually in journals after a cooperative activity is an effective way to build in accountability. Writing in journals also enhances Intrapersonal intelligence. For this reason, many of the activities in *Exploring the Rain Forest* include journal suggestions. An added benefit is that journals can be used as an assessment tool.

How can we make a difference?

After studying about problems associated with rain forest destruction, it's important to help students find ways to make a difference. They can write letters to elected officials about their concerns, learn the value of recycling, and talk to their parents about not buying products that contribute to rain forest destruction.

However, one of the most satisfying ways students can make a difference is to become involved an Adopt-an-Acre campaign such as the one sponsored by the Earth Foundation. In this project, students sell T-shirts to help raise money to save the rain forest. For each 10 T-shirts sold, one acre of rain forest is saved. At the end of the school year, participating schools receive a videotape showing the area that they helped save and a full report of how the money was spent. Every year the Earth Foundation targets one area of endangered rain forest to purchase and set aside as a nature preserve. In recent years students have raised over a million dollars and saved almost 100,000 acres throughout the world. For more information contact the Earth Foundation (see Rain Forest Resources).

As a teacher, you can make a difference by creating an atmosphere of excitement and wonder about the rain forest. Fortunately, creating this excitement is easy when you use cooperative learning structures and multiple intelligence lessons. Let this book be your passport to an exciting rain forest adventure!

The Eight Intelligences
At-A-Glance

Students are attracted to or skilled with:

Verbal/Linguistic
- Reading
- Writing
- Speaking

Logical/Mathematical
- Numbers
- Computations
- Logical sequences
- Abstract symbols

Visual/Spatial
- Art
- Maps
- Diagrams
- Arrangements

Musical/Rhythmic
- Music
- Rhythm
- Singing

Bodily/Kinesthetic
- Motor skills
- Sports
- Body Language
- Movement

Naturalist
- Plants
- Animals
- Classifying
- Organizing

Interpersonal
- People
- Other's Feelings
- Personal Skills

Intrapersonal
- Feelings
- Values
- Reflection

Chart of Activities & Curriculum Areas

Activity (page)	Mathematics	Science	Social Studies	Health	Reading	Language Arts	Art	Music
1. We Wonder (3)		●				●		
2. Action Letters (7)		●				●		
3. Tropical Products (13)		●		●				
4. Sentence Practice (17)						●		
5. Jungle Mapping (19)			●				●	
6. Word Power (25)					●	●		
7. Who Knows? (29)		●	●		●			
8. Rain Forest Factoids (31)	●	●		●				
9. Layers of Life (35)	●	●			●	●	●	
10. Comparing Climates (45)	●	●	●					
11. Dictionary Word Sort (53)					●	●		
12. Tropical Treasure Hunt (57)		●	●		●	●		
13. Medical Mysteries (63)				●	●			
14. Tropical Poetry (71)					●	●		●
15. Rain Forest in a Bag (77)		●						
16. Vivid Vocabulary (81)					●	●	●	
17. It's About Time (89)	●				●			
18. Same-Different (93)		●					●	
19. Jigsaw Story Mapping (97)					●	●		

Chart of Activities & Curriculum Areas (cont)

Curriculum Area

Activity (page)	Mathematics	Science	Social Studies	Health	Reading	Language Arts	Art	Music
20. Comparing Kids (101)		●	●		●	●		
21. Erosion Experiment (105)		●						
22. Words in a Word (109)					●	●		
23. Traveling Showdown (111)	●							
24. Amazing Animals (115)		●			●	●	●	
25. Mystery Animal (121)		●				●		
26. Food Chain Fun (123)		●						
27. Create a Creature (129)		●				●	●	
28. Write Around (133)						●		●
29. Math Talk (139)	●	●						
30. Causes and Effects (143)		●			●			
31. Rain Forest Dilemma (147)			●		●	●		
32. Agreement Circles (151)		●	●					
33. Save the Rain Forest (153)		●	●		●	●		
34. Tropical Tunes (155)						●		●
35. Puppet Shows (159)		●				●	●	
36. Concept Mapping (163)	●	●	●	●	●	●		

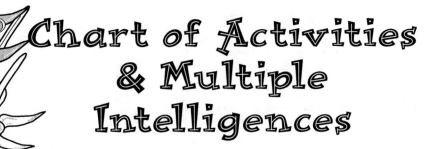

Chart of Activities & Multiple Intelligences

Activity (page)	Verbal/Linguistic	Logical/Mathematical	Visual/Spatial	Musical/Rhythmic	Bodily/Kinesthetic	Naturalist	Interpersonal	Intrapersonal
1. We Wonder (3)	●						●	●
2. Action Letters (7)	●		●				●	●
3. Tropical Products (13)	●	●	●			●	●	
4. Sentence Practice (17)	●					●	●	
5. Jungle Mapping (19)	●	●				●	●	
6. Word Power (25)	●					●	●	
7. Who Knows? (29)	●		●		●	●	●	
8. Rain Forest Factoids (31)	●	●				●	●	
9. Layers of Life (35)	●	●	●		●	●	●	●
10. Comparing Climates (45)	●	●	●				●	●
11. Dictionary Word Sort (53)	●	●			●	●	●	
12. Tropical Treasure Hunt (57)	●		●				●	●
13. Medical Mysteries (63)	●						●	●
14. Tropical Poetry (71)	●			●		●	●	
15. Rain Forest in a Bag (77)	●		●		●	●	●	
16. Vivid Vocabulary (81)	●		●			●	●	
17. It's About Time (89)	●	●	●			●	●	
18. Same-Different (93)	●	●				●	●	
19. Jigsaw Story Mapping (97)	●	●	●			●	●	

Chart of Activities & Multiple Intelligences (cont)

Curriculum Area

Activity (page)	Verbal/Linguistic	Logical/Mathematical	Visual/Spatial	Musical/Rhythmic	Bodily/Kinesthetic	Naturalist	Interpersonal	Intrapersonal
20. Comparing Kids (101)	●	●	●			●		
21. Erosion Experiment (105)	●	●	●		●	●	●	
22. Words in a Word (109)	●		●		●	●	●	
23. Traveling Showdown (111)	●	●			●	●	●	
24. Amazing Animals (115)	●		●		●	●	●	
25. Mystery Animal (121)	●	●			●	●	●	●
26. Food Chain Fun (123)	●		●	●	●	●	●	●
27. Create a Creature (129)	●		●			●	●	●
28. Write Around (133)	●			●		●	●	
29. Math Talk (139)	●	●						
30. Causes and Effects (143)	●	●	●			●	●	
31. Rain Forest Dilemma (147)	●					●	●	
32. Agreement Circles (151)	●		●		●	●	●	●
33. Save the Rain Forest (153)	●		●			●	●	
34. Tropical Tunes (155)				●			●	
35. Puppet Shows (159)	●	●	●	●	●	●	●	●
36. Concept Mapping (163)	●		●				●	●

Chart of Structures & Activities

Structure	Activity
1. Agreement Circles	32
2. Blackboard Share	4, 22
3. Find Someone Who	7
4. Jigsaw	9, 12, 16, 19, 31
5. Mix-Freeze-Group	26
6. Mix-Freeze-Pair	8, 12
7. Numbered Heads Together	17
8. Pairs Compare	3, 10, 20, 30
9. Pair Discussion	4, 33
10. Pair Project	24
11. RallyRobin	20
12. RallyTable	3, 14, 20, 22
13. RoundRobin	1, 6, 12, 14, 16, 19, 28, 34
14. RoundTable	1, 2, 11, 14, 17, 27, 28, 33, 36
15. Same-Different	18
16. Showdown	23
17. Spend-A-Buck	28, 35
18. Stand-N-Share	3, 30, 33, 34
19. Team Discussion	12, 25, 36
20. Team Interview	25
21. Teammates Consult	5, 13, 29
22. Team Project	2, 10, 13, 14, 15, 26

Exploring the Rain Forest by Laura Candler • **Kagan Publishing** • 1 (800) 933-2667 • www.KaganOnline.com

Exploring the Rain Forest Pre/Post Test

1. What makes up a tropical rain forest?

   _____
   _____
   _____
   _____
   _____
   _____
   _____
   _____

2. Why are rain forests important?

   _____
   _____
   _____
   _____
   _____
   _____
   _____
   _____

Exploring the Rain Forest Pre/Post Test
(continued)

3. What problems are caused by cutting down rain forests?

4. What is our responsibility regarding the rain forest?

We Wonder

Students complete a Know-Wonder-Learned chart and share their knowledge and questions with team members.

ACTIVITY 1

Steps...

Cooperative Structure
- RoundRobin
- RoundTable

Content Areas
- Science
- Language Arts

Materials
- We Wonder charts (4 per team)
- Poster paper or large construction paper (1 per team)
- Crayons or markers

Multiple Intelligences
- Interpersonal
- Intrapersonal
- Verbal/Linguistic

1. Introduce Chart

Ask students to number off within their teams from 1 to 4. Give each person a Know-Wonder-Learned chart or have them draw one in their journal. *"Today as we begin our Rain Forest unit, I want you to think about what you already know about the tropics. I also want you to think of things you wonder about the rain forest — questions that you would like answered as we complete our unit of study."*

2. Individuals Write

"I want you to list everything that you already know about the rain forest under the word 'Know' on the chart." Allow as much time as students need for this.

3. RoundRobin

"Now take turns telling your team what you know. Starting with Student #1, each person will share what they have written."

4. Individuals Write

"As you listened to your teammates, you probably thought of many questions you would like answered. What would you like to know about the rain forest? Under the word 'Wonder,' write the questions that you have about tropical rain forests."

5. RoundRobin

"Take turns reading your questions to your team. This time start with Student #2 and continue clockwise around the team."

6. RoundTable Posters

Give each team a piece of poster paper and a box of crayons or markers.

ACTIVITY 1 continued

We Wonder

☺ Hints and Variations

Q - Matrix - If your class is familiar with the Q-Matrix materials available from *Kagan Cooperative Learning*, use the Q-Matrix grid in Step 4. Students can refer to the question prompts as they write their 'Wonder' questions about the rain forest.

Journal Idea

Immediately after students complete the "Know" and "Wonder" sections of their chart, have each student write three to five "I wonder" questions in their own journal. Ask them to leave a space for the answers, which they may fill in throughout the unit.

"Student #1, please write 'We Wonder' at the top of the page and then pass it to the person on your left. Now in RoundTable fashion, each of you take turns listing your best questions under the heading on your team poster. We will display your posters in the room to help guide us during our study of the rain forest."

7. Discover Answers

"As we study about the rain forest, try to discover the answers to your questions. Each time you find an answer, write it in the 'Learned' column of your personal Know-Wonder-Learned chart. Be prepared to share your answers at the end of our unit."

Sample Team Poster

We Wonder
- What kinds of animals live in the rain forest?
- Why are people cutting them down?
- Does it really rain every day in a rain forest?

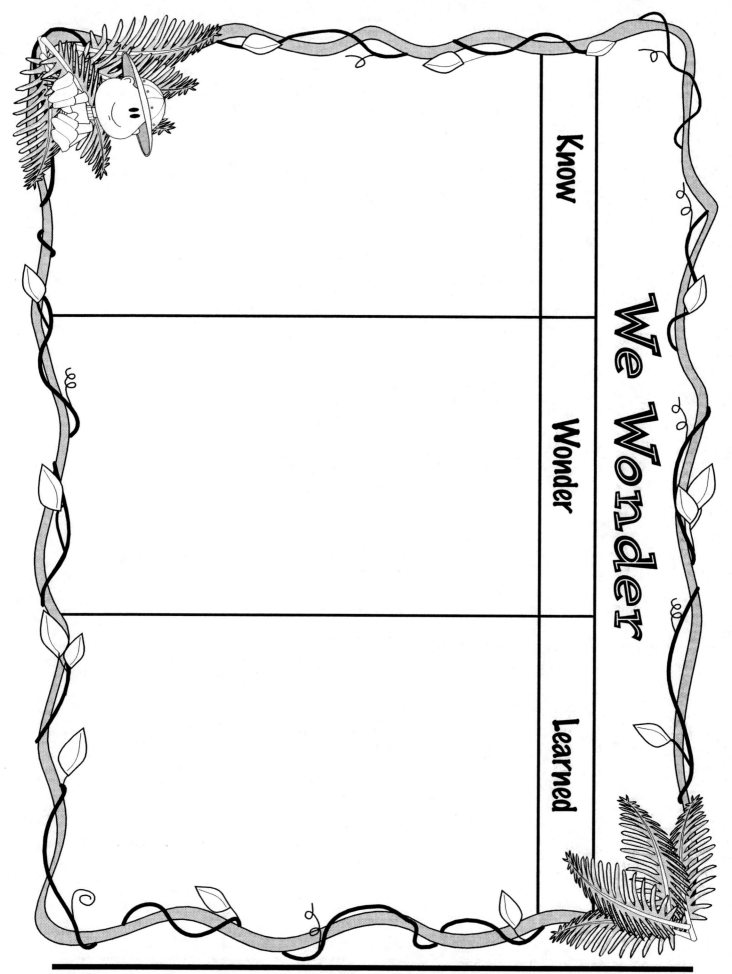

Action Letters

Students write letters to rain forest conservation agencies to find out how they can help save the tropics.

ACTIVITY 2

Steps...

Cooperative Structures
- Think-Pair-Share
- RoundTable

Content Areas
- Science
- Language Arts

Materials
- Transparency of **Sample Letter & Envelope**
- 2 or 3 copies of **Rain Forest Organization addresses**
- **Editing Role Cards** (1 set per team)
- Writing paper
- Envelopes & stamps (students may bring these from home)
- Dictionaries (1 per team)

Multiple Intelligences
- **Verbal/Linguistic**
- **Visual/Spatial**
- **Interpersonal**
- **Intrapersonal**

1. Think-Pair-Share
Put up the Sample Letter & Envelope transparency. Ask students to think, *"How is a business letter different from a friendly letter?"* After several seconds say, *"Pair up with a teammate and discuss your ideas."* After a few minutes call on students to share their ideas.

2. RoundTable Ideas
"Today we will write letters to organizations that work to save the rain forests. What do you want to write in your letters? What information would you like to request? Before we begin, I would like your team to list ideas. Student #1, take a piece of paper and write one idea. Pass the paper to the left so the next person can add an idea. Keep passing the list and adding ideas until I call time."

3. Distribute Addresses
While students are listing ideas, cut apart the Rain Forest Organization addresses and give each student one slip. You may have to give several students the same address.

4. Individuals Write
Keep the sample on the overhead and have students write their rough drafts independently. After they finish, have them follow the example to correctly address their envelopes. Remind them to include only the necessary postal information, not the Internet and e-mail addresses.

5. RoundTable Edit
Give each team member one of the four Editing Role Cards (Letter Form Checker, Spelling Checker, Sentence Checker, and Envelope Checker). Give the directions: *"Now we will work as a team*

ACTIVITY 2 continued
Action Letters

to edit our letters. Each team member has a different job to do as he or she reads each letter. Begin by passing your own letter, address slip, and envelope to the person on your left. Read the new letter carefully, according to your role. Make corrections or write comments if you find problems. Do not pass the letter again until I call time." Call time when most students seem ready. Have students continue passing and editing until everyone has seen all letters.

6. Mail Letters

Have students bring stamps from home so that they can mail their letters. As a courtesy, have students include a self-addressed, stamped envelope if they are requesting information or materials. Allow 4 to 6 weeks for a response from most organizations.

Variations

- **E-mail Letters** – Students may enjoy e-mailing their letters rather than sending them through the postal service. However, caution students against requesting information that's readily available on the organization's Web site.

- **Taking a Stand** – After students become familiar with rain forest problems, have them choose an issue and organize a letter-writing campaign to take action. The Rainforest Action Network (**www.ran.org**) provides up-to-date information about specific rain forest issues and includes addresses for these types of action letters. Students can also write to elected officials, encouraging them to support legislation that will help preserve rain forests.

Rain Forest Organizations

Conservation International
2501 M. Street NW, Suite 200
Washington, DC 20037
(202) 429-5660
www.conservation.org

National Wildlife Federation
8925 Leesburg Pike
Vienna, VA 22184
(703) 790-4000
www.nwf.org

Rainforest Relief
P.O. Box 150566
Brooklyn, NY 11215
(718) 832-6775
http://host.envirolink.org/rainrelief
e-mail: relief@igc.apc.org

Earth Foundation
5151 Mitchelldale, Suite B-11
Houston, TX 77092
(800) 5MONKEY
www.earthfound.com

The Nature Conservancy
Adopt An Acre Program
1815 North Lynn Street
Arlington, VA 22209
(703) 841-5300
www.tnc.org

Sierra Club
85 Second Street, Second Floor
San Francisco, CA 94105
(415) 977-5500
www.sierraclub.org
e-mail: information@sierraclub.org

Earth's Birthday Project
P.O. Box 1536
Santa Fe, NM 87504-1536
(800) 689-4438
www.earthsbirthday.org
e-mail: earbirpro@aol.com

Rainforest Action Network
221 Pine Street, Suite 500
San Francisco, CA 94104
(415) 398-4404
www.ran.org
e-mail: rainforest@ran.org

Tropical Rainforest Coalition
461 Park Ave., Ste. #4
San Jose, CA 95110
(408) 496-9412
www.rainforest.org
e-mail: in@nanospace.com

Environmental Defense Fund
257 Park Avenue South
New York, NY 10010
(800) 684-3322
www.edf.org
e-mail: school coordinator@edf.org

Rainforest Alliance
65 Bleecker Street
New York, NY 10012
(212) 677-1900
www.rainforest-alliance.org

World Wildlife Fund
1250 24th Street, NW
Washington, DC 20037-1175
(202) 293-4800
www.worldwildlife.org
e-mail: wwfus@worldwildlife.org

Sample Letter & Envelope

115 Douglas Avenue
Fayetteville, NC 28314
January 1, 1998

Earth Foundation
5151 Mitchelldale, Suite B-11
Houston, TX 77092

Dear Sir or Madam:

   I am a 5th grade student at E. E. Miller Elementary School. My class is studying about the tropical rain forest. I was hoping you could send me some information about plants and animals of the rain forest. I would especially like some pictures. I also want to know what problems are caused by people cutting down rain forests and what I can do to help.
   Please send any information to the address above. Thank you for your time!

                              Sincerely,
                              Jessica Rowland
                              Jessica Rowland

Jessica Rowland
115 Douglas Avenue
Fayetteville, NC 28314

                        Earth Foundation
                        5151 Mitchelldale, Suite B-11
                        Houston, TX 77092

Editing Role Cards

Sentence Checker

Things to Check

☐ Are there any run-on sentences?
☐ Did you find any sentence fragments?
☐ Is the wording clear and easy to understand?

Envelope Checker

Things to Check

☐ Is the return address correct?
☐ Is the mailing address correct?

Editing Role Cards

Spelling Checker

Things to Check

- ☐ Is the address spelled correctly?
- ☐ Are words spelled correctly in the letter?

Letter Form Checker

Things to Check

- ☐ Is the date in the correct place?
- ☐ Is the inside address placed correctly?
- ☐ Is each section punctuated correctly?

Tropical Products

Students observe a variety of products and infer that the items come from the rain forest.

ACTIVITY 3

Cooperative Structures
- Pairs Compare
- RallyTable
- Stand-N-Share

Content Areas
- Science
- Health

Materials
- **Tropical Products** page (1 per class)
- Samples of chocolate, coffee, and cinnamon
- A variety of other rain forest products
- Thinkpad paper (scrap paper)

Multiple Intelligences
- Verbal/Linguistic
- Logical/Mathematical
- Visual/Spatial
- Naturalist
- Interpersonal

Steps...

1. Gather Products
Use the Tropical Products page to help guide you as you gather samples of rain forest products. You will need coffee, chocolate, and cinnamon as well as a variety of other items.

2. Compare Coffee and Chocolate
Pair students for this RallyTable activity. Show the class samples of coffee and chocolate. Do not tell students that these items come from the rain forest! Say *"What do these two items have in common? Take turns with your partner listing all the ways coffee and chocolate are alike. I'll give you two minutes to write your ideas."*

3. Pairs Compare
"Now compare your answers with another pair. Take turns naming the ways and checking off the items on your lists."

4. Team Challenge
"As a team, try to think of even more ways that coffee and chocolate are alike. Take turns adding any new ideas to your lists. Both lists must contain the same items at the end of the discussion."

5. Stand-N-Share
Designate a Reporter from each team and ask that person to stand. *"I will ask each Reporter to name one way that chocolate and coffee are alike. If you have that idea on your list, place a check beside it so you won't name that item when I call on you. When you have no more items on your list, sit down."* Continue asking for responses until all Reporters are sitting down.

6. Add Cinnamon
Show the students a sample of cinnamon. Ask *"What do cinnamon, chocolate, and coffee all have in common? Using your original list, take turns crossing off any ideas that don't hold true for all*

Exploring the Rain Forest by Laura Candler • *Kagan Publishing* • 1 (800) 933-2667 • www.KaganOnline.com

Tropical Products

8. Discuss Common Link

After all the products are on display, ask volunteers to share ideas for what all the items have in common. If no one guesses that they all come from the rain forest, reveal the common link. Tell them that even though many of the items are now grown on plantations, they all originally came from the rain forest.

Journal Idea

Ask students to reflect on the activity by writing in their Rain Forest Journals. "List at least five rain forest products that you or your family use. Describe how your life would be different without these things."

three items. If you think of any additional similarities, add them."

7. Add Other Products

Continue adding rain forest products one at a time. Be sure to include some nonfood items like rubber or bamboo. Each time, ask students to discuss ways these items are similar. Have them cross off attributes that no longer hold true for all items.

Sentence Practice

Students practice grammar skills by correcting sentence errors. They compare with a partner and discuss their corrections as a class.

Steps...

ACTIVITY 4

Cooperative Structures
- Blackboard Share
- Pair Discussion

Content Area
- Language Arts

Materials
- Rain Forest Sentences for Practice (1 per class)

Multiple Intelligences
- Verbal/Linguistic
- Naturalist
- Interpersonal

1. Individuals Write

Write one Rain Forest Sentence on the board each day. *"Read the sentence on the board. You will find many errors which may include spelling mistakes as well as other types of grammar errors. Write the sentence correctly in your journals. You may look words up in a dictionary or even use your language arts books to check rules of grammar. Do your own work. You will discuss your ideas later with a partner."*

2. Pairs Discuss

Assign partners for this step. *"Now compare your sentence with your partner's. Discuss the corrections you made. You have two minutes to make any further corrections."*

3. Blackboard Share

Randomly choose a student from the class to come forward and make corrections. Be sure to have him or her give reasons for each change. As the student makes corrections to the sentence, ask students to make corrections in their journals.

Exploring the Rain Forest by Laura Candler • **Kagan Publishing** • 1 (800) 933-2667 • www.KaganOnline.com

Rain Forest Sentences for Practice

1. Have you ever ben too a rane forest.
2. If not, youve probly herd of rain forests some people call them jungels.
3. Me and my mother had went to the amazon rain forest last year.
4. We seen many colorfull birds insects and flours.
5. We seen bats bees and butterflys darting from flower to flower.
6. Polinated flowers become frute that will be ate by parrots tocans insecs bats and other animals.
7. Air plants grows in the tops of trees they soke up food and watter with there leafs and roots.
8. One tipe of air plant are called a bromeliad it look like the top of a pinapple.
9. We use rain forest Products when we eat brekfast water house plants or fly in a plain.
10. Corn rice and tomatos was first discoverd growwing in a tropical Rain Forest.
11. Tea cofee suger brazil nuts and bannanas growed in jungel climates.
12. Ronald said "one of the best knowed plants is the ruber tree its milky sap is called latex.
13. "How are latex made into rubber" asked Sally?
14. I dont no replied Ronald. we havn't studyed that in sceince class yet."
15. "Will you try to find out how ruber is made asked Sally?
16. Chemicles in leaves flowers and seeds is used to make everything from prefumes to chewwing gum.
17. Hunderds of people take medecines witch contain chemicals from rain forest plants.
18. These plants can kill gurms reduce fever lower blood pressure and relax musles.
19. Sientists will visit the amazon rain forest in brazil to lern more about these plants.
20. Are lives would be verry difrent if rain forests was destroid.

Jungle Mapping

In teams, students color world maps to show the locations of major tropical rain forests.

ACTIVITY 5

Cooperative Structure
- Teammates Consult

Content Areas
- Social Studies
- Art

Materials
- Overhead transparency of **Teammates Consult Directions** (1 per class)
- **Jungle Mapping** worksheets (1 per student)
- **Jungle Mapping Direction Cards** (1 set per team)
- Scissors
- Crayons or colored pencils (1 set per person)

Multiple Intelligences
- Verbal/Linguistic
- Logical/Mathematical
- Visual/Spatial
- Naturalist
- Interpersonal

Steps...

1. Distribute Materials

Give each student one Jungle Mapping map and colored pencils or crayons. Give each team one set of Direction Cards to cut apart. Ask them to put the cards in numerical order and stack them face up in the center of the team. Place the transparency of the Teammates Consult Directions on the overhead.

2. Model Activity

Stand next to a team and explain the steps of Teammates Consult. As you describe each step, refer to the overhead transparency and have the model team go through the motions of completing that step. "*Each of you will color a map to show important features of the earth as well as the locations of major rain forests. Begin by placing your coloring materials in the center of the team. Student #1 is the first Leader and reads the first Direction Card aloud. Everyone discusses the directions. You may refer to your social studies book or an atlas if needed. Then the Leader asks, 'Does everyone know what to do?' If everyone answers yes, you each color your map **without talking.** If someone is confused, continue discussing the directions until everyone knows what to do. After you finish, put your coloring materials back in the center of the team to show you are ready. Then Student #2 becomes the next Leader and reads the next Direction Card. Continue rotating Leaders throughout the activity.*"

3. Color Maps

Teams color their maps by following the instructions on the Direction Cards. Monitor the progress of each team to make sure they are staying together. Encourage them to consult classroom maps or their social studies books as they follow the directions.

ACTIVITY 5 continued

Jungle Mapping

Journal Idea

In their journals, have students respond to this question: *"What do you notice about the location of most rain forests?"* Make sure that students understand that most rain forests are found near the equator.

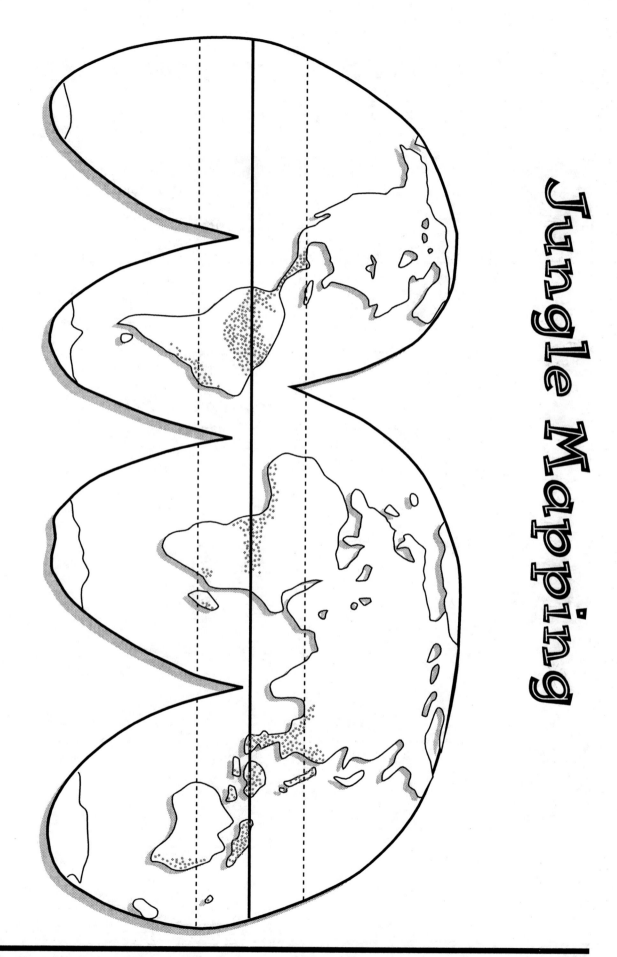

Jungle Mapping Direction Cards

1. Label the equator and trace it in red.

2. Find the Tropic of Cancer and the Tropic of Capricorn. Trace over them in orange.

3. Label the seven continents.

4. Make a purple dot on the map to show where you live.

5. Color the rain forests green.

6. Color the continents brown.

7. Label the four oceans.

8. Color the oceans blue.

Jungle Mapping

Teammates Consult Directions

1. Stack the Jungle Mapping Direction Cards **face up in order** in the center of the team.

2. Everyone puts down their crayons (or colored pencils).

3. The Leader reads the first direction card aloud and everyone discusses how to color the map.

4. The Leader asks, "Does everyone know how to color this part of the map?"

5. If anyone answers "No," continue the discussion.

6. When everyone is ready, they pick up their crayons.

7. **Without talking,** everyone colors the map according to the first direction card.

8. Everyone puts down their crayons when finished.

9. Next person becomes new Leader and reads the second direction card. Rotate Leaders for each card.

Crayons Down → Talking Allowed
Crayons in Hand → No Talking

Exploring the Rain Forest by Laura Candler • *Kagan Publishing* • 1 (800) 933-2667 • www.KaganOnline.com

Word Power

In teams, students build their rain forest vocabulary. Then individuals write stories to share with their team.

ACTIVITY 6

Cooperative Structure
- RoundRobin

Content Areas
- Reading
- Language Arts

Materials
- Rain Forest Vocabulary Word List
- Word Power Vocabulary Cards (1 set per team)
- Scissors
- Word Power Role Cards (1 set per team)

Multiple Intelligences
- Verbal/Linguistic
- Naturalist
- Interpersonal

Steps...

1. Distribute Materials
Give each team one set of Word Power Cards with vocabulary words already printed on them. Have students work together to cut the cards apart and stack them face down in the middle of the team. Then give each team a set of Role Cards to cut apart and fold into "tents." Number students on each team 1 to 4 and have them distribute the Role Cards accordingly.

2. Model Activity
As you describe the activity, stand beside a team and direct them to model the steps. *"Today you will practice spelling and using rain forest words correctly. To begin, Student #1 picks a card up from the stack and reads the word aloud. Student #2 spells the word. Student #3 defines the word. Finally, Student #4 uses the word in a sentence. After the first round, rotate the Role Cards to the left and follow your new directions. Continue rotating until your team has practiced all vocabulary words."*

3. RoundRobin
As students complete the Word Power activity, monitor to be sure they are giving the correct responses. Encourage students to question any spellings, definitions, or sentences which seem incorrect.

Journal Idea
In their rain forest journals, have students write a short story using as many spelling words as possible. Allow 10 to 15 minutes for writing. Then allow students to RoundRobin read their stories to their team.

Exploring the Rain Forest by Laura Candler • Kagan Publishing • 1 (800) 933-2667 • www.KaganOnline.com

Rain Forest Vocabulary

Animals

anteater	hawk
jaguar	lizard
macaw	iguana
boa constrictor	quetzal
caterpillar	python
howler monkey	ocelot
toucan	sloth
butterfly	bat
hummingbird	chameleon

Products

chocolate	bamboo
banana	wicker
coffee	sugarcane
coconut	cocoa
cinnamon	cashews
medicine	pineapple
vanilla	chewing gum

Plants

orchid	mushrooms
bromeliad	palm
buttress	banana tree
liana vines	cacao tree
ferns	snake plant
philodendron	kapok tree
strangler fig	

Miscellaneous

deforestation	tropical
green house effect	oxygen
global warming	carbon dioxide
environment	emergent layer
poison	canopy
endangered	understory
extinct	forest floor
ecologist	camouflage
botanist	

Word Power Vocabulary Cards

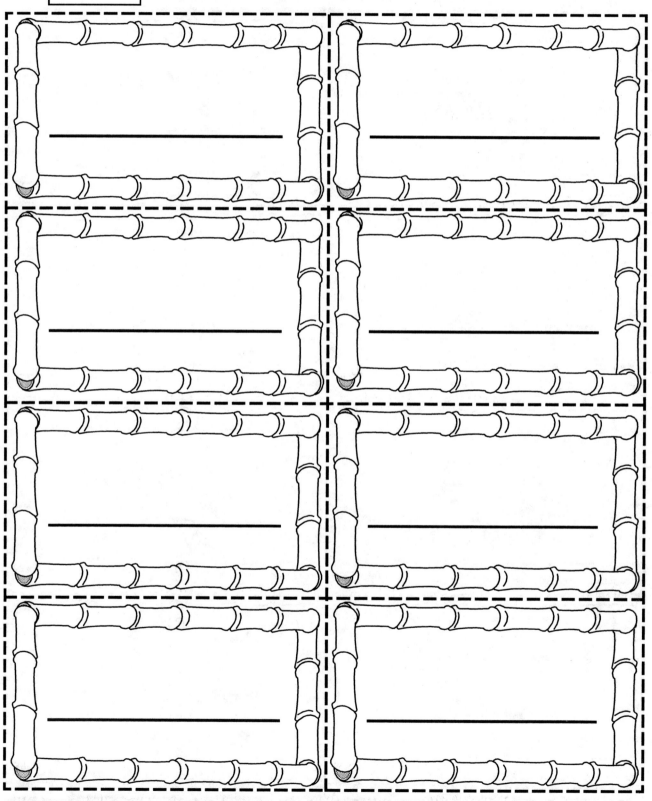

Word Power
Role Cards

#1	#2
Read the word aloud	Spell the word
#3	#4
Define the word	Use the word in a sentence

Who Knows?

Students listen to a children's book describing the rain forest and its problems. They review what they learned by playing Find Someone Who.

ACTIVITY 7

Cooperative Structure
- Find Someone Who

Content Areas
- Science
- Social Studies
- Reading

Materials
- Find Someone Who worksheets (1 per person)

Literature Links
Rain Forest Secrets, Why Save the Rain Forest?, or *Nature's Green Umbrella* (or other nonfiction children's book about the rain forest)

Multiple Intelligences
- **Verbal/Linguistic**
- **Visual/Spatial**
- **Bodily/Kinesthetic**
- **Naturalist**
- **Interpersonal**

Steps...

1. Read Aloud
Read aloud a nonfiction book about the rain forest, or show a filmstrip or video describing the rain forest and its problems. Depending on the age of your students, you may want them to take notes as you read or show the filmstrip.

2. Find Someone Who
Give each person one Find Someone Who worksheet. *"Now we will review the ideas you have learned. Each of you will move about the room trying to find someone who knows the answers to the questions. As you pair with a partner, ask a question from the worksheet. If they know the answer, write it on the lines. Then ask them to check it for accuracy and sign their name. Switch roles and allow them to ask you a question. When you are both finished, thank each other and find new partners. Return to your seats when you have all the parts of your worksheet completed."*

3. Check Answers
When everyone is seated, quickly check the answers to the questions. Call on individuals to volunteer what they have written for each item.

Journal Idea
Ask students to write five new things they learned about the rain forest from this activity.

Exploring the Rain Forest by Laura Candler • **Kagan Publishing** • 1 (800) 933-2667 • www.KaganOnline.com

Find Someone Who...

Knows what tropical rain forests look like.	Knows where tropical rain forests are located.
Name _____	Name _____
Can describe the climate of a tropical rain forest.	Can name 3 animals that live in the rain forest.
Name _____	Name _____
Can name 3 products that come from the rain forest.	Knows why rain forests are important.
Name _____	Name _____
Knows 2 reasons rain forests are being cut down.	Knows 2 problems caused by cutting down tropical rain forests.
Name _____	Name _____

30 *Exploring the Rain Forest* by Laura Candler • **Kagan Publishing** • 1 (800) 933-2667 • www.KaganOnline.com

Rain Forest Factoids

Students mix around the room and pair with classmates. They discuss rain forest facts involving fractions and percents, restating those statistics in their own words.

ACTIVITY 8

Cooperative Structure
- Mix-Freeze-Pair

Content Areas
- Mathematics
- Science
- Health

Materials
- **Rain Forest Factoids** transparencies

Literature Links
The Rain Forest Book by Scott Lewis

Multiple Intelligences
- Verbal/Linguistic
- Logical/Mathematical
- Naturalist
- Interpersonal

Steps...

1. Review Concepts
Review terminology relating to fractions and percents. Use examples from the classroom such as, "Everyone is here today. What percent is that? What if two people were absent? How could we write that as a fraction? How could we write it as a percent?"

2. Introduce Activity
"When you read about the rain forest, you often discover interesting facts about the plants and animals that live there. Sometimes these facts seem confusing because they are given as percents. However, if you talk about what each fact means and state it in your own words, you'll find them very easy to understand."

3. Explain Factoids
Place the Rain Forest Factoids transparency on the overhead. "Let's read and think about the first example. Rain forests cover seven percent of the earth's land surface. What does that mean?" Allow think time, and then say, "Since percent means 'part of 100,' imagine all the land on the earth divided into 100 parts. Rain forests cover only seven of those parts. Is that more or less than half?"

4. Students Mix
"Now you are going to discuss more rain forest facts with other students in the class. Stand up and mix around the room quietly until I say 'Freeze.'"

5. Freeze and Pair
After a few seconds say, "Freeze! When I say 'Pair,' make eye contact with someone near you and move close to that person to become their partner. Pair!"

6. Pairs Discuss
"Listen as I read the next rain forest fact. Discuss what it means in your own words. Be ready for me to call on you to share your ideas with the class."

Rain Forest Factoids

7. Repeat
Repeat the Mix-Freeze-Pair sequence with each new rain forest fact.

> **Journal Idea**
> Have students choose the two most interesting facts they learned and write about them in their journals.

Part 1

Rain Forest Factoids

- Rain forests cover seven percent (7%) of the earth's land surface.

- Fifty percent (50%) of the rain forests that were once on the earth have already been destroyed.

- Rain forests are home to half of all living things.

- The Amazon Rain Forest makes up one-third (1/3) of all rain forests found on earth.

- Pharmacologists have identified 3,000 plants as having cancer-fighting properties. Seventy-percent (70%) of them grow in rain forests.

- Fewer than 1 percent (1%) of all tropical rain forest plants have been studied for their possible use in medicine.

Adapted from: *The Rain Forest Book* by Scott Lewis

Part 2
Rain Forest Factoids

- In the last 40 years, two-thirds (2/3) of the rain forest in Central America have been cleared.

- About 40 species of birds live in the rain forests of Hawaii. Unfortunately, of those 40, three out of four (3/4) species are classified as endangered.

- Nearly 100 percent (100%) of Hawaii's invertebrate species are *endemic.* That is, they occur naturally no where else on the earth.

- Bats are important because they eat fruits and spread the seeds throughout the rain forest. Nearly nine-tenths (9/10) of the seeds in the rain forest are dispersed by bats.

- Scientists estimate that nearly one in six (1/6) rain forest plant species can provide products other than timber.

Adapted from: *The Rain Forest Book* by Scott Lewis

Layers of Life

By taking part in a Jigsaw activity, students learn about the 4 layers of rain forest life. Then each person draws their layer to scale and adds it to the team's picture of the rain forest.

ACTIVITY 9

Cooperative Structure
- Jigsaw

Content Areas
- Mathematics
- Science
- Reading
- Language Arts
- Art

Materials
- **Rain Forest Layer** descriptions (7 or 8 copies of each per class)
- **Layers of Life Jigsaw Notes** page (1 per person)
- **Poster Labels** (1 set per team)
- 9" x 12" white construction paper (1 per person)
- Colored construction paper or poster board, at least 12" x 18" (1 per team)
- Crayons or colored pencils
- Rulers and scissors (at least 1 of each per team)
- Glue (1 bottle per team)
- Assorted books and pictures of the rain forest
- **Rain Forest Layers Quick Quiz** (1 copy per class)

Multiple Intelligences
- Verbal/Linguistic
- Logical/Mathematical
- Visual/Spatial
- Bodily/Kinesthetic
- Naturalist
- Interpersonal
- Intrapersonal

Steps...

Getting Ready

To complete this lesson, students must understand the concept of scale drawings. If they have had no prior experience with scale drawings, refer to your mathematics textbook for a full lesson. For this activity, students will be assigned to four "Expert Group" stations where they will learn about one layer of rain forest life (Emergent Layer, Canopy, Understory, and Forest Floor). Prepare one Expert Group Station for each of the four rain forest layers. At each station include coloring materials, 9" x 12" sheets of white construction paper, rulers, scissors, and assorted rain forest books or pictures. Place 7 or 8 copies of the appropriate Rain Forest Layer description at each station.

1. Review Scale Drawing

Draw a stick person on the board. Pair students and say, *"Suppose I want to draw this person to scale using a scale of 1 inch equals 2 feet. If the person is 6 feet tall in real life, how tall would I draw him on paper? Think . . . now discuss your ideas with your partner. Both of you, use a ruler and try drawing this stick figure to scale."* Check student drawings and give additional examples if needed.

2. Form Expert Groups

Have students in teams number off from 1 to 4. Give each person one copy of the Layers of Life Jigsaw Notes page. Say, *"Scientists have divided rain forest life into four layers from top to bottom. Today you will become an expert on one rain forest layer. Student #1 will learn about the Emergent Layer. Student #2 will study about the Canopy. Student #3 will learn about the Understory, and Student #4 will become an expert on the Forest Floor. You will each move to one of four stations, study about your layer, and draw an illustration of that layer."*

ACTIVITY 9 continued

Layers of Life

3. Take Notes

Students move to their assigned expert group stations. Each person gets one copy of the description page for that layer, but only one person reads the information aloud. Say, *"When you return to your teams you will teach the others about your layer. To help you do this, take notes about the height of each layer, as well as the plants, animals, and amount of sunlight found in your layer. Record your notes on the appropriate section of your Jigsaw Notes page. At the end of this lesson, each of you will take an individual quiz to see how much you learned about all four rain forest layers."*

4. Illustrate Layers

While in expert groups, students decide how to draw their layer of the rain forest using a scale of 1 inch equals 20 feet. Each person draws that layer on white construction paper, making sure the paper is held *vertically*. Students may refer to outside resources such as books and pictures to add details to their pictures. Remind students to draw all plants and animals to scale. Then students studying the Canopy, Understory, and Forest Floor cut their drawings out. The students studying the Emergent Layer keep the entire paper intact and bring it back to the team.

5. Teams Reunite

When students have finished their drawings, ask them to return to their base teams. Give each team one 12" x 18" sheet of colored construction paper or a piece of poster board. Say, *"Now you will teach each other about your layer of the rain forest. As you work, you will create a 3-D poster of the rain forest by stacking your pictures."*

6. Teach Emergent Layer

Ask all Student #1's, who have the Emergent Layer, to glue their picture vertically in the center of the their team page. Say, *"Student #1, use your notes to teach your team about the Emergent Layer. Be sure to tell your team about the amount of sunlight in that layer, as well as the types of plants and animals that are found there. The rest of the team should take notes about the Emergent Layer on their own note-taking page."*

7. Add Other Layers

"Now place a thin bead of glue along the bottom edge of the Emergent Layer picture. Student #2, place your drawing of the Canopy on top of the first layer, making sure you line up the bottom edges. After you do this, teach your team about your layer. Everyone else take notes." Follow the same procedure for the Understory and Forest Floor, in that order. Only the bottom edges should be glued, with the top of the Canopy and Understory free to flap forward.

8. Complete Posters

Give each team one set of Poster Labels. Say, *"To finish your team picture, add the heading and other labels. Work together to cut out the Poster Labels. Glue the heading at the top, the scale at the bottom, and the arrows in their correct locations on the side."*

9. Administer Quick Quiz

Have teams put away their posters during the quiz. Ask each person to take out a sheet of paper and number it from 1 to 8. Call out the questions (or place a transparency of the test on the overhead projector). This quiz can be graded, but remember that each student's performance is based on the presentations of their team. Use the grades for informal assessment only.

Hints and Variations

Leapfrog Jigsaw - You may want to teach this lesson using a variation called "Leapfrog Jigsaw." To do this, call one Expert Group at a time to meet with you, instead of having all groups meet simultaneously. Assign the other students seatwork during these meetings (such as reading rain forest books or solving math problems). The advantage to Leapfrog Jigsaw is that you are free to guide each Expert Group through their lesson and scale drawing session.

Journal Idea

Say, "In your journals, write a summary of what you have learned about each of the four rain forest layers."

Sample Rain Forest Layer Project

Rain Forest Layers
Quick Quiz

1. Which of the layers receives only 3% of the sunlight?

2. Which layer is also called the Umbrella Layer?

3. Where does the harpy eagle make its home?

4. Which layer contains more plant and animal life than any other?

5. Where do leaf cutter ants make their home?

6. What layer is just below the canopy?

7. Which layer contains trees that may be over 200 feet tall?

8. In which layer will you find the cacao trees whose pods are used for making chocolate?

> Canopy   Understory
> Emergent Layer   Forest Floor

Layers of Life
Jigsaw Notes

1. Emergent Layer	2. Canopy
	|//
3. Understory	4. Forest Floor

Emergent Layer

Description

Emergent Layer trees are the ones that rise up above the thick layer of the Canopy. Emergent trees may be over 200 feet tall, but there are often only one or two of them per acre of rain forest. These trees receive plenty of sunlight, and they are exposed to changing weather conditions and air movement. Only a few animals brave the towering heights of these trees. The harpy eagle makes its home here, swooping down into the canopy below to seize unsuspecting monkeys, sloths, or snakes. Many insects live in the emergent layer, including the shimmering blue Morpho butterfly.

Scale Drawing Directions

Trees in the Emergent Layer are often 220 feet tall. Using a ruler, draw two tall trees as shown using a scale of 1 inch equals 20 feet. Draw the trees to scale on your white paper. Start your measurement from the bottom edge of your paper. Do not cut out the trees. Use a blue crayon to shade the area behind the trees.

Scale: 1 inch = 20 feet

Canopy

Description

The Canopy, sometimes called the Umbrella Layer, rises from 60 to 160 feet above the rain forest floor. The Canopy receives much more sunlight than the lower layers, and the air is much less humid. Many types of air plants, called epiphytes, grow on the branches of the Canopy trees. These plants often look like pineapple tops and don't have roots that reach the ground; instead, they get their nutrients from the moist air. Tree frogs lay their eggs in small pools of water trapped by these plants. The trees are alive with colorful birds, mammals, reptiles, and amphibians that make their homes far above the ground. Howler monkeys, three-toed sloths, toucans, hummingbirds, lizards, and boa constrictors enjoy the sunny environment of the Canopy.

Scale Drawing Directions

The tops of the trees in the Canopy are often 160 feet high. Using a ruler, draw a layer of trees that stretches from one side of your white paper to the other. Use a scale of 1 inch equals 20 feet. Draw the trees as shown. Start your measurement from the bottom edge of your paper. Then cut across the tops of the trees and throw away the top portion of the paper.

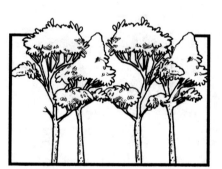

Scale: 1 inch = 20 feet

Understory

Description

The Understory is the layer just above the forest floor, rising to about 60 feet above the ground. Very little sunlight filters through the branches above, so this part of the rain forest is dark and shady. The air is always moist here. Small trees, bushes, and woody vines called lianas make up the plant life of the Understory. Cacao, the tree from which cocoa is made, grows at this level. Because it is dark, not many flowers bloom in the Understory. Spider monkeys swing from branch to branch, and animals such as the flying fox and fruit bat swoop between the trees. Boa constrictors, tree frogs, and iguana are especially suited for life in the Understory.

Scale Drawing Directions

Trees in the Understory are between 20 and 60 feet tall. Using a ruler, draw a layer of small trees across the bottom of your plain white paper. Use a scale of 1 inch equals 20 feet. Start your measurement from the bottom edge of the page. Cut across the tops of the trees and throw away the upper portion of the paper.

Scale: 1 inch = 20 feet

Forest Floor

Description

The Forest Floor is very dark and damp. Only about 3 percent of the sunlight filters through the treetops above. Everything is constantly dripping with moisture. The soil is not very rich so the forest floor is actually quite open. There are small plants such as bushes, ferns, young trees, and mushrooms. Rotten logs lie across the forest floor, but they decay quickly in the damp moisture. Leaf cutter ants scurry across the forest floor carrying pieces of leaves that are ten times their size. Anteaters roam freely, making a meal of ants and termites. Jaguars and other predators prowl through the darkness looking for unsuspecting prey.

Scale Drawing Directions

Small plants, dead trees, and large bushes make up the Forest Floor. Using a scale of 1 inch equals 20 feet, draw a 5 foot tall person to scale at the bottom of your plain white paper. Then draw a layer of bushes, logs, and plants to scale. Cut across the top of your drawing and throw away the upper part or save it for another project.

Scale: 1 inch = 20 feet

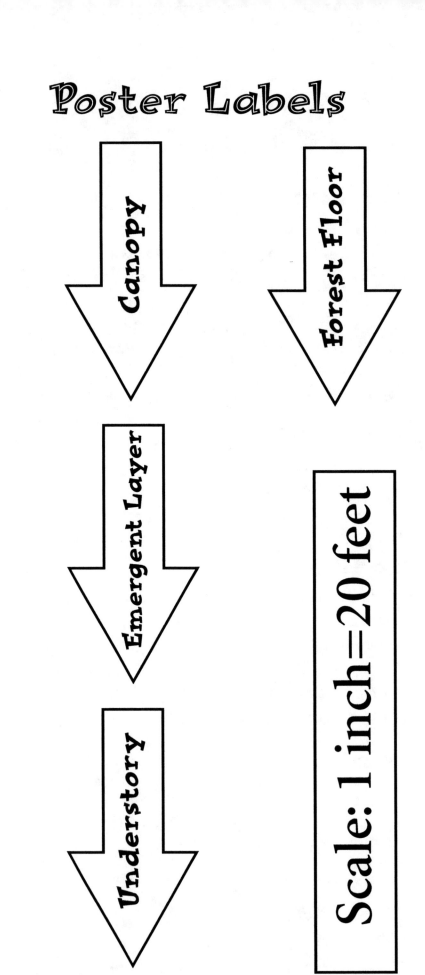

Comparing Climates

Students work in pairs to graph monthly rain forest weather data. They compare that data to weather patterns in their own community.

ACTIVITY 10

Steps...

Cooperative Structures
- Pairs Compare
- Think-Pair-Share

Content Areas
- Mathematics
- Science
- Social Studies

Materials
- **Weather Data** worksheet (1 per pair)
- **Comparing Precipitation** graph (1 per pair)
- **Comparing Temperature** graph (1 per pair)
- Colored pencils (1 box per team)
- 1 Transparency of each blank graph
- Transparency pens in 2 colors

Multiple Intelligences
- **Verbal/Linguistic**
- **Logical/Mathematical**
- **Visual/Spatial**
- **Interpersonal**
- **Intrapersonal**

Getting Ready

Before starting this activity, locate the necessary weather data for your city and a rain forest city. You will need the monthly precipitation and temperature averages for each location. The easiest method of finding this information is to visit the WorldClimate Web site at *www.worldclimate.com* which provides weather data for thousands of cities. Complete the blank Weather Data charts before duplicating them for your class. If you are unable to obtain this information, you may want to use the weather data for Raleigh, North Carolina and Manaus, Brazil which is provided on a sample chart.

1. Think-Pair-Share

"What do you think the climate of a rain forest is like? How hot or cold would you expect it to be compared to where we live? What kind of rainfall would you expect?" Allow a few moments of individual think time, and then have students pair with a partner to discuss the questions. Finally, call on students to share their ideas with the class.

2. Introduce Activity

Divide each team of four into pairs. Give each pair one Weather Data worksheet, one Comparing Precipitation graph, and two different colored pencils. Place the overhead transparency of the Precipitation Graph on the overhead projector. *"Let's find out how the climate of the rain forest compares with our climate. Today you are going to work with a partner to create climate graphs from the information found on these charts. Let's start by comparing the precipitation in our area to that of a the Amazon Rain Forest in Brazil."* If a map is available, ask students to locate Manaus, Brazil.

Exploring the Rain Forest by Laura Candler • Kagan Publishing • 1 (800) 933-2667 • www.KaganOnline.com

Comparing Climates

3. Graph Local Precipitation

"Each of you take a colored pencil and fill in one of the boxes in the graph key. Today you will create a double bar graph comparing the rainfall in Brazil to the rainfall we receive. One person will read out the precipitation data for our area first. The other person will draw and color the bars according to the color key below the graph." Demonstrate how to color the bar showing local January precipitation. Monitor and assist where needed. Be sure students are leaving room for the second bar on each month.

4. Graph Rain Forest Precipitation

"Now switch roles. The other person will call out the rain forest precipitation data and his or her partner will color the bars in a different color according to the key." Demonstrate using the other color on the overhead transparency.

5. Pairs Compare Graphs

After everyone has completed their double bar graphs say, "Compare your graph with your teammates. Do they look the same? What have you learned about the rainfall in our area as compared to the rain forest?"

6. Graph Local Temperatures

Place the Comparing Temperature overhead transparency on the projector. Give each pair a Comparing Temperature graph. Say, "Now you and your partner will create a double line graph to compare our average monthly temperature to temperatures in the rain forest. Use two different colored pencils to color the key at the bottom of the graph. One person will call out the monthly local temperatures while his or her partner plots the points and connects them with straight lines." Demonstrate with one color on the overhead transparency.

7. Graph Rain Forest Temperatures

"Now switch roles as you did before. One person calls out the rain forest temperatures while the other person plots the points and connects them. Be sure to use a different color pencil. Don't worry if the two lines cross." Demonstrate on the overhead transparency.

8. Pairs Compare Graphs

"Compare your double line graph with the one created by your teammates. Do they look the same? What did you learn about temperatures in the rain forest as compared to our temperatures?"

9. Think-Pair-Share

"Why do you think rain forest climates are different from ours? What might cause those differences?" Allow think time and then pair students to discuss the questions. Finally, have students share their thoughts with the class. Be sure to discuss factors such as distance from the equator and amount of vegetation.

Variation

Students Research Data - If Internet computers are available in your classroom or a lab setting, distribute blank Weather Data charts and let students work in teams to visit the WorldClimate Web site and record the data on their own.

Journal Idea

Have students summarize what they learned about the climate of the rain forest. Are there seasons in the tropics? Ask them to imagine that winter came to the rain forest. How would this affect the plants and creatures that live there?

Rain Forest
Weather Data
Manaus, Brazil

Month	Average Precipitation (inches)	Average Temperature (°F)
January	10	79
February	10	79
March	12	79
April	11	79
May	8	79
June	4	79
July	3	80
August	2	81
September	3	82
October	4	82
November	6	81
December	9	80

Local
Weather Data
Raleigh, NC

Month	Average Precipitation (inches)	Average Temperature (°F)
January	4	41
February	4	43
March	4	52
April	3	60
May	4	68
June	4	75
July	5	78
August	4	77
September	3	72
October	3	61
November	3	52
December	3	44

Source: worldclimate.com

Local Weather Data

Month	Average Precipitation (inches)	Average Temperature (°F)
January		
February		
March		
April		
May		
June		
July		
August		
September		
October		
November		
December		

Rain Forest Weather Data

Month	Average Precipitation (inches)	Average Temperature (°F)
January		
February		
March		
April		
May		
June		
July		
August		
September		
October		
November		
December		

Exploring the Rain Forest by Laura Candler • *Kagan Publishing* • 1 (800) 933-2667 • www.KaganOnline.com

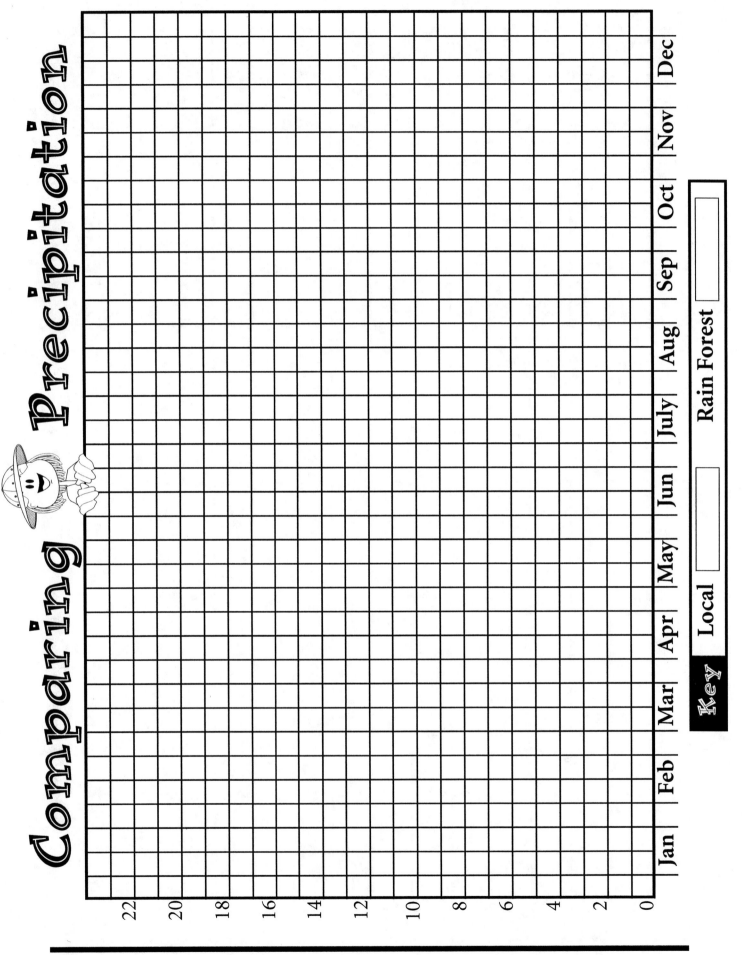

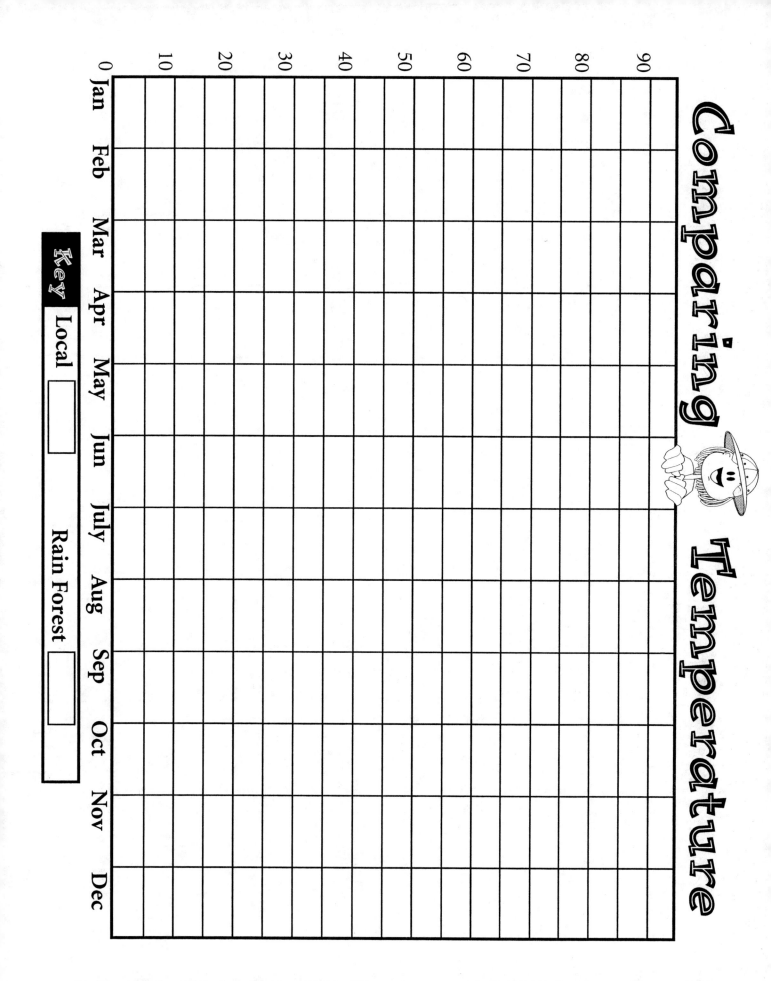

Dictionary Word Sort

In teams, students use dictionary skills to sort rain forest word cards.

ACTIVITY 11

Cooperative Structure
- RoundTable

Content Areas
- Reading
- Language Arts

Materials
- **Dictionary Word Sort** game boards (1 per team)
- **Guide Words and Entry Words** blackline masters (2 pages - 4 sets - per team)
- Scissors

Multiple Intelligences
- Verbal/Linguistic
- Logical/Mathematical
- Bodily/Kinesthetic
- Naturalist
- Interpersonal

Steps...

1. Prepare Materials
Cut each Guide Words and Entry Words page in half. Give each team one game board and one half-page of guide words and corresponding entry words. (Only give students one half-page set at a time to prevent mixing up the sets.) "*Work together to cut out the guide word rectangle and the entry word cards. Place the guide words at the top of your game board and stack the entry words face down in the lower box at the bottom of the page.*"

2. Sort Words
Now have students take turns sorting the cards in RoundTable fashion. "*Student #2, turn over the top entry card and read it to your team. Imagine that you are looking this word up in a dictionary. Look at the guide words on your game board and decide if the entry word would come before the page with those guide words, on the page, or after the page. Put the entry word in the correct location. Everyone else, look at the placement and give Student #2 a thumbs-up if you agree. If you don't agree, explain why. Student #3 will turn over the next card, and so on until all cards are sorted.*"

3. Repeat
As each team finishes sorting a set of cards, check their answers. Remove the guide words and entry words for each set before giving a new set of cards. Students repeat the activity with each set of cards.

Journal Idea
Give the last set of cards to each person individually. (Duplicate additional sets or have students take turns.) Ask students to make three columns in their journal and head them "Before," "On," and "After." Have students sort the word cards and list the words in the appropriate columns.

Exploring the Rain Forest by Laura Candler • Kagan Publishing • 1 (800) 933-2667 • www.KaganOnline.com

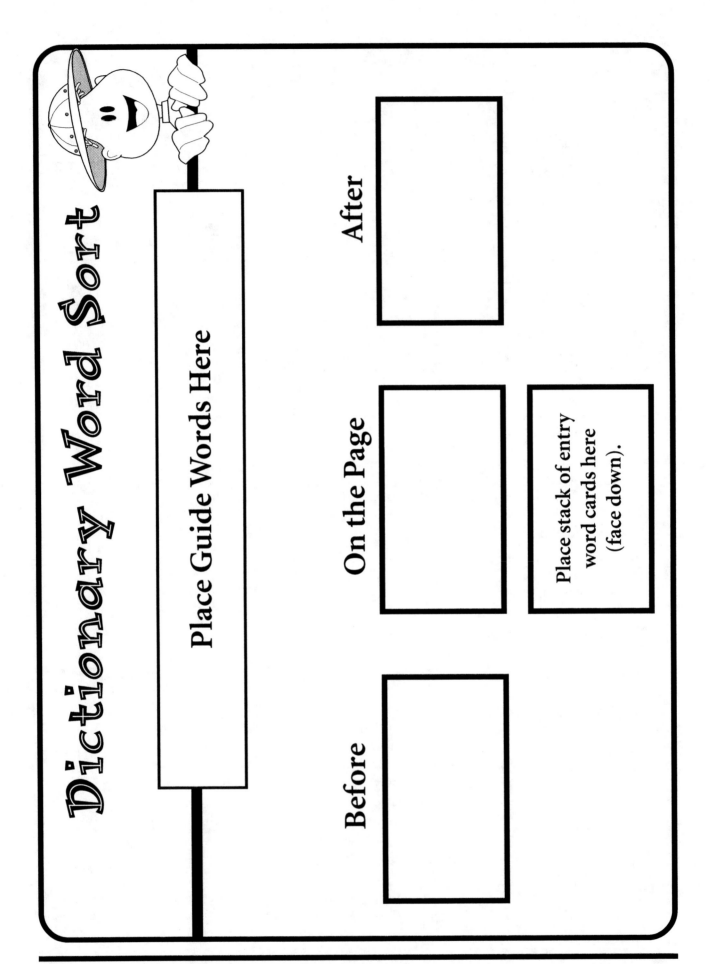

Guide Words & Entry Words

sloth – tree frog

shrew	toucan	tropical
snake	sugarcane	salamander
termite	tapir	tanager

jungle – lime

iguana	liana vine	lion
monkey	latex	jaguar
lemon	lizard	nutmeg

Guide Words & Entry Words

orchid - peanut

orange	pepper	ocelot
parrot	owl	palm
pineapple	papaya	periwinkle

army ant - botanist

avocado	anteater	coconut
beetle	bromeliad	butterfly
boa	banana	buttress

Tropical Treasure Hunt

Students participate in an Internet Treasure Hunt, using clues to discover information about rain forests.

ACTIVITY 12

Steps...

Cooperative Structures
- Jigsaw
- Mix-Freeze-Pair
- RoundRobin
- Team Discussion

Content Areas
- Science
- Social Studies
- Reading
- Language Arts

Materials
- Computer with Internet access
- **Tropical Treasure Hunt** note pages (1 set per person)
- **Speak Out!** worksheet (1 per person)

Multiple Intelligences
- Verbal/Linguistic
- Visual/Spatial
- Interpersonal
- Intrapersonal

Internet Link
Tropical Treasure Hunt
http://home.att.net/~candlers/tropical.htm

1. Introduce Activity

An Internet treasure hunt involves searching the Internet to find the answers to specific questions. Generally, the questions and related Internet links are organized on one Web page which encourages students to remained focused on the activity. Explain to students that they will be working in teams to explore questions about tropical rain forests. Log on to the Internet and demonstrate how locate the Tropical Treasure Hunt page (*http://home.att.net/~candlers/tropical.htm*). Bookmark the site, since students will want to return to this page many times during their treasure hunt. Scroll through the page and explain that students will be answering the questions by searching the Web sites listed at the bottom of the page.

2. Explain Jigsaw

Divide the class into Base Teams of four students each, and number students off from one to four. *"For this activity, we will use a study method called 'Jigsaw.' These teams of four are your Base Teams. Within your Base Teams, each team member will only be responsible for finding the answers to two questions and will become an "expert" on these areas. You will work with other experts to learn about your two areas. Then you will meet back together to share that information with the other members of your Base Team."*

3. Form Expert Groups

Give each student a copy of the two-page Tropical Treasure Hunt handout. When forming Expert Groups, refer to the geometric shapes around each number on the worksheet. Within each Base Team, Student #1's are Circles, Student #2's are Triangles, Student #3's are Diamonds, and Student #4's are Pentagons. To form Expert Groups, ask students

Activity 12 continued

Tropical Treasure Hunt

to move to four different corners of the room designated Circles, Triangles, Diamonds, and Pentagons.

4. Research Answers

By referring to the shapes, students can see the questions they are responsible for answering. (The Circles will answer 1 and 5, the Triangles are responsible for 2 and 6, the Diamonds will respond to 3 and 7, and the Pentagons will look for answers to 4 and 8.) Allow the members of each Expert Group to work together as they search the Internet to answer the two questions. Have them record their answers on their worksheets, and remind them to cite their Internet sources for each answer. If you don't have four Internet computers, you may want to work out a rotation system to allow each team adequate research time at the computer. You might also want to consider using a program such as Web Whacker to harvest the sites needed during the treasure hunt.

5. Return to Base Teams

When students have had adequate time to explore their two questions, have them return to their original Base Teams.

6. RoundRobin

In RoundRobin fashion, have students share the information they learned. Starting with Question #1, Student #1 explains the answer while the others jot notes on their handout. Then Student #2 shares the information concerning Question #2 and so on. Allow plenty of time for this sharing session.

7. Team Discussion

Pose each of the following questions to the class, one at a time. Allow time for teams to discuss their ideas before sharing their thoughts with the class.
- *Why are rain forests important to us, even if we don't live near one and might never visit one?*
- *What do you think would happen if all rain forests were destroyed?*
- *What do you think should be done about the rain forest problem?*

8. Individuals Write

Give each person one copy of the Speak Out! page. *"Think about the creatures of the rain forest. Imagine yourself as a rain forest animal who has been given the power to speak. What would you say to humans about the rain forest problem? Be sure to tell why the rain forest is important and what you think should be done about the problem."* Artistic students may wish to draw their own animals and speech bubbles rather than using the worksheet provided.

9. Mix-Freeze-Pair

Finally, ask students to stand up and quietly mix around the room with their animal speeches in hand. Call out "Freeze!" and then "Pair!" When all students are in pairs, have them read their speeches to each other. If time allows and students are interested, repeat the Mix-Freeze-Pair sequence to allow them the opportunity to share their speech with another class member.

Extensions

- **Participate in a Web Quest** — Web Quests are more complex than Treasure Hunts, but they are perfect for cooperative learning investigations. *Under the Umbrella of the Tropical Rainforest* is an excellent Web Quest created by Carole Girouard, a high school Media Specialist in New Bedford, Massachusetts. Since the activity is divided into four parts, Jigsaw would be an ideal structure to use with this investigation. To find this Web Quest on the Internet, point your browser to *http://www.gnbvoc.mec.edu/rainforest*.

- **Create Your Own Internet Activities** — Teachers interested in creating their own Internet activities will enjoy visiting a Web site sponsored by Pacific Bell called Filamentality *(http://www.kn.pacbell.com/wired/fil/)*. Without any knowledge of Web site construction, visitors to the site can create their own Treasure Hunts, Web Quests, Hotlists, and more. Better yet, those activities are available immediately on the World Wide Web at no charge.

Tropical Treasure Hunt

Questions 1-4

1. Where in the world are rain forests located?

2. What is the climate of a rain forest like?

3. What kinds of plants and animals live there?

4. What are the layers in the rain forest? Name and describe each one.

Tropical Treasure Hunt

Questions 5-8

5. Why are rain forests important?

6. Why are people cutting down rain forests?

7. What are some problems caused by deforestation?

8. What are at least three things kids can do to save the rain forest?

Speak Out!

Name _____

Medical Mysteries

Students read an article about medical secrets of the rain forest. Using Teammates Consult, they answer questions about the article.

ACTIVITY 13

Steps...

1. Think-Pair-Share

Pair students for this discussion. Tell them that scientists know that many rain forest plants can be used to cure sickness and disease. Ask *"How do you think scientists learn about the medical value of rain forest plants and animals?"* Give them 10 seconds of think time, then have them talk over their ideas with their partner. Finally, call on students to share with the class.

2. Individuals Read

Give each student a copy of "In Search of Jungle Secrets" and say, *"This article describes how one scientist discovers medical mysteries of the rain forest. Read the article silently to learn how Mark Plotkin uncovers these jungle secrets."*

3. Teammates Consult

Place a large cup in the center of each team. Give each student one copy of the Medical Mysteries worksheet and place the Teammates Consult directions on the overhead projector. Stand next to a team and say, *"Today you are going to work with your team to answer the questions on the worksheet. This activity is called 'Teammates Consult' because you will talk over your ideas for each question before writing your own answer. Watch and listen as I have this team demonstrate the steps. Student #1 on this team will be the first Leader. The Leader will rotate for each round."*

Lead the team through the steps outlined on the Teammates Consult direction page. When everyone understands the directions, students may begin discussing the first question. The directions may be confusing at first, so walk around and make sure students are completing the activity correctly. For individual accountability, students must not be allowed to talk while they are actually

Cooperative Structure
- Teammates Consult
- Think-Pair-Share

Content Areas
- Health
- Reading

Materials
- Copies of **"In Search of Jungle Secrets"** (1 per person)
- **Medical Mysteries** worksheet (1 per person)
- **Teammates Consult** directions (1 transparency per class)
- Large cup for pencils (1 per team)

Literature Links
The Shaman's Apprentice by Mark Plotkin and Lynne Cherry

Multiple Intelligences
- Verbal/Linguistic
- Interpersonal
- Intrapersonal

ACTIVITY 13 continued

Medical Mysteries

writing on their worksheets. Make sure team members are staying together and that some students are not racing through the worksheet on their own. Patient waiting is an important social skill during this activity.

Variation

- **RallyTable** – Duplicate one copy of the article for each pair of students. Instead of having them read it individually, have them take turns reading each paragraph to their partner.

Extension Activities

- **Research Ethnobiology** – Since this article was written, Dr. Plotkin has left Conservation International. He left that organization to collaborate with other scientists in creating *Amazon Conservation Team*. Visit their Web site (www.ethnobotany.org) to learn more about the field of Ethnobiology and Dr. Plotkin's ongoing work.

- **Read Aloud** – Locate a copy of *The Shaman's Apprentice*, a recent book by Mark Plotkin and Lynne Cherry. This is the story of Kamanya, a young tribesman who dreams of becoming his tribe's next shaman. His dream is threatened when a foreigner arrives who appears to have medicine that is even stronger than the shaman's.

- **E-mail Dr. Plotkin** – Have a class representative or team of students write a letter to Dr. Plotkin. Before writing the letter, have the class brainstorm questions and comments they would like included in the letter. After composing the letter, have the students visit *Amazon Conservation Team* Web site and send the message using the e-mail link provided.

Journal Idea

As students finish their worksheets, have them respond to this question in their journals: *"Would you like to have Mark's job? Why or why not?"*

Medical Mysteries

Name _____

1. Why does Mark Plotkin travel each year to the South American rain forest?
   _____
   _____
   _____

2. Who are shamans and why are they important to rain forest tribes?
   _____
   _____
   _____

3. How does Mark get medical information from the shamans?
   _____
   _____
   _____

4. What are some of the dangers Mark faces in his work?
   _____
   _____
   _____

5. What plan does Mark have for saving the rain forest?
   _____
   _____
   _____

Medical Mysteries

Teammates Consult Directions

1. Team members have identical worksheets.

2. Everyone places their pencils in the team cup.

3. The Leader reads first question and begins a discussion about possible answers.

4. The Leader asks, "Is everyone ready?"

5. If the answer is "No," continue the discussion

6. When everyone is ready, they pick up their pencils.

7. **Without talking**, everyone writes the answer to the first question. (Answers may be different.)

8. Everyone places pencils back in the cup.

9. Next person becomes the new Leader. Continue rotating leaders for each question.

> Pencils In Cup → Talking Allowed
> Pencils In Hand → No Talking

In Search of Jungle Secrets

MARK PLOTKIN travels thousands of miles each year. He flies from his Washington, D.C., office of Conservation International to the South American rain forests. There he faces poisonous snakes, sharp-toothed *piranha* fish, and deadly diseases. And all so he can collect a bunch of plants and talk to the people who know them best.

Why?

Medicine. "Many of our medicines originally came from plants," he explains. "And as we learn about more plants, we can use them to make new medicines."

OK. So why isn't Mark in Washington, studying plants in a lab?

"It's faster to go to people who already know the plants' secrets," he explains.

He's not talking about scientists. He means *shamans*. Medicine men. "Witch Doctors."

Experts in the Jungle

Most tribes have a shaman — a person other members of the tribe go to when they're sick or troubled. Their shamans treat them with chants, magic, and plants.

The *plants* are what Mark is interested in talking to the shamans about. The shamans' knowledge about plants has been handed down from the old to the young for thousands of years. All those generations of shamans used and tested each plant. "That's more testing than scientists do in the lab," Mark says.

As an example, he points to the *rosy periwinkle*. This small flower is used for medicine by people in Madagascar. (That's a big island off the southeast coast of Africa.) The plant is now being used around the world to treat a kind of cancer often found in children.

Here was a case (and there are many others) where the local shamans knew more about some plants than the scientists did. So Mark wants to talk to the shamans to find out what they know.

But he has to move fast: As jungle people learn more about the outside world, fewer of them use the shamans for healing. And Mark has found few young people trying to become shamans. Much of what shamans have learned about plants is dying out with them.

*Reprinted from the February 1990 issue of **Ranger Rick** magazine, with the permission of the publisher, the National Wildlife Federation. Copyright 1990 by the National Wildlife Federation.*

In Search of Jungle Secrets (continued)

Sneaking up on Secrets

So what does Mark do — find a shaman and say, "Hey, tell me about your plants"?

"No way," Mark says. "A lot of this information is secret. And shamans have no reason to trust me, an outsider."

Mark has to find clever ways to get the information instead. Often he does it by using what he already knows about the plants. Then he can guess at what they might be used for. He'll say, "In my country, we use that plant for back pain." The shaman might disagree, saying, "No, that's used to treat elbow sprains." Mark collects the plant and writes down, *elbow sprains*. Then he'll ask, casually, "So what do *you* use for back pain?" If the shaman tells him, he's learned about *two* plants!

Mark has tried out a number of these jungle plants on himself and his friends. They don't always work. And he's taking a big risk — the plant might even make a disease worse! But he's seen many of the plants work on the rain forest people. So he thinks the plants are worth trying.

Right now, he's excited about a fungus that seems to cure earaches. And he's studying another plant that may get rid of a disease called athlete's foot.

Deadly Poisons

Mark knows it's important to go looking for possible new medicines. But it's not always easy. The places he explores are hot and humid. And the insects there can be so thick that "sometimes you can't eat without getting a mouthful of them," he says.

Then there's the food. Mark's learned to eat things like snake meat (which he says is good with Tabasco sauce) and a kind of rodent the jungle people boil and eat. He claims it's delicious.

But he also deals with things that can cause far more than a stomach ache — like poisons. The tips of hunters' darts and arrows are smeared with these poisons. Mark knows they kill quickly. So he is careful to try to be good friends with the hunters.

But he's very interested in how the poisons are made, because some medicines started with plant poisons. Take *curare* (cure-AREee), which is used to make muscles relax. It comes from a plant brought to Europe 150 years ago by an explorer. The explorer found Amazonian Indians using it as poison on their arrow tips.

*Reprinted from the February 1990 issue of **Ranger Rick** magazine, with the permission of the publisher, the National Wildlife Federation. Copyright 1990 by the National Wildlife Federation.*

In Search of Jungle Secrets (continued)

Longing to Explore

When Mark was little, did he dream about roaming the jungle, eating boiled rodents, and watching out for poison arrows?

Well, yes — sort of. "I always wanted to be an explorer," he says. He remembers hanging around the swampy woods near his New Orleans home, looking for snakes and turtles.

And he dreamed of growing up to see "something nobody'd ever seen before — something you don't find in the shopping malls. Most people I know have outgrown that longing to explore," he says. "But I never grew up!"

Saving the Rain Forests

Now Mark's working to save the wild places he loves exploring. And he knows of a clever plan.

"I'm telling medicine companies that there are plants in the rain forests that they can use," he explains. "These kinds of plants usually can't be grown on farms. So if medicine companies want them and want to find new plant medicines, they'll have to help save the rain forests so that they can keep up supplies."

Pretty sneaky, huh? Wait, there's more: He knows about plants that grocers and food manufacturers can use too. Things like *guanabana* (gwa-NAH-bah-nah), which tastes almost like pineapple custard. And *lulo* (LOO-low), a yellow-orange fruit that Mark says is used to make a delicious drink.

There are other plants in the rain forests Mark thinks could make money for companies — companies that make all kinds of things from vegetable oil to clothing. To make that money, the companies must help keep the rain forests safe and healthy.

It's an idea worth exploring, from a real explorer.

*Reprinted from the February 1990 issue of **Ranger Rick** magazine, with the permission of the publisher, the National Wildlife Federation. Copyright 1990 by the National Wildlife Federation.*

Tropical Poetry

Students listen to rain forest poetry and write rain forest images for each of their five senses. Then they combine those images into a team poem.

ACTIVITY 14

Cooperative Structures
- RallyTable
- RoundRobin
- RoundTable
- Think-Pair-Share

Content Areas
- Reading
- Language Arts
- Music

Materials
- Tape of rain forest music or sound effects
- Pictures, books, videotapes, or filmstrips showing rain forest scenes
- Colored pencils (1 per person)
- **Sensational Poetry** Idea Maps (1 per pair)
- **Rain Forest Poetry** form (1 per team)
- **Poetry Praisers** (1 per person)
- Scissors (at least 1 per team)

Literature Links
Welcome to the Green House by Jane Yolen

Multiple Intelligences
- Verbal/Linguistic
- Musical/Rhythmic
- Naturalist
- Interpersonal

Steps...

1. Read Aloud
Before using this lesson, make sure students have had exposure to books, filmstrips, and videotapes showing scenes from the rain forest. *"Relax, and take an imaginary journey with me to the rain forest. As I read, picture the rain forest in your mind and pretend you are walking through the jungle."* Play rain forest music or sound effects as you read *Welcome to the Green House* by Jane Yolen.

2. Discuss Poetry
Use Think-Pair-Share to discuss the concept of "poetry." Show students the pages of *Welcome to the Green House* and explain that the book is a long poem illustrated with rain forest artwork. Ask students to think: *"How is poetry different from other forms of writing?"* Then have them pair: *"Turn to a partner and take turns naming as many differences as you can."* Finally, call on students to share their ideas. During the class discussion, explain that poems usually rely on strong images and use lines and stanzas instead of sentences and paragraphs. Make sure they understand that poems don't have to rhyme.

3. Write Images
Give each pair of students one "Sensational Poetry" idea map and two different colored pencils. *"Imagine once again that you are walking through the rain forest. Look around…what do you see? Listen carefully…what do you hear? Use all your senses to experience the rain forest. Each of you use a different colored pencil and take turns with your partner writing strong images for each sense."* (Each pair must write at least one image for each sense, but they may write more than one if they wish.)

4. RoundRobin Images
"Now share your images with the rest of the team. Take turns reading one image from your paper until all images have been read aloud."

ACTIVITY 14 continued
Tropical Poetry

5. Write Poems

Give each team one Rain Forest Poetry form and have them write a team poem in RoundTable fashion. *"You are going to combine your best images into one team poem. To do this, you will pass the paper in RoundTable fashion. Student #3 will begin by completing the first phrase 'As I walked through the tropical rain forest I saw…' The team may help with ideas on how to word the stanza. Then the paper is passed to Student #4* who completes the next phrase 'As I walked through the tropical rain forest I heard . . .' and so on. When you have completed all five images, the last person reads the entire poem to the team. Think of an effective way to end the poem. Write a title on top. Revise and edit your poem until everyone is happy with it."

6. Present Poems

Give each person one sheet of Poetry Praisers. Have students cut apart the praiser slips on the dotted lines. Let each team choose a Reader to present their team poem to the class. Ask each person in the audience to write a compliment or praiser about each team's poem after it is read. One person on each team serves as the Mailcarrier and delivers the praisers to the team at the end of the lesson.

Journal Idea

Have students write their team poem in their journals. Encourage them to personalize the poem by adding or changing the images to make the stanzas even stronger.

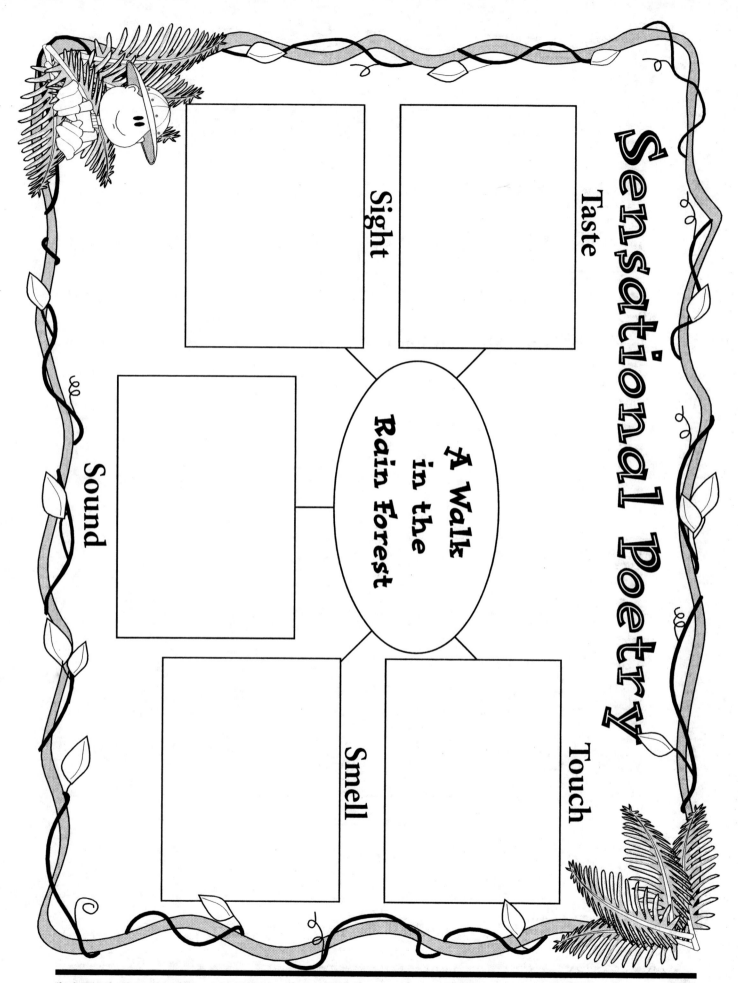

Rain Forest Poetry

Poem Title _____

As I walked through the tropical rain forest
I saw _____
_____

As I walked through the tropical rain forest
I heard _____
_____

As I walked through the tropical rain forest
I smelled _____
_____

As I walked through the tropical rain forest
I tasted _____
_____

As I walked through the tropical rain forest
I touched _____
_____

As I walked through the tropical rain forest
I felt _____
_____

Poets _____
_____

Poetry Praisers

To: _____
I like your poem because…

From: _____

To: _____
Your poem gets a "thumbs up" because…

From: _____

To: _____
Your poem is superb because…

From: _____

To: _____
I enjoyed your poem because…

From: _____

To: _____
What I like about your poem is…

From: _____

To: _____
The best thing about your poem is…

From: _____

Exploring the Rain Forest by Laura Candler • **Kagan Publishing** • 1 (800) 933-2667 • www.KaganOnline.com

Rain Forest in a Bag

ACTIVITY 15

Students plant a variety of seeds in large plastic zip bags to create mini rain forests.

Steps...

1. Introduce Activity
"Today we are going to learn more about the rain forest by growing our own miniature rain forests in plastic bags. Each team will plant seeds in one bag and each day we will record our observations about our rain forests. This will be a Team Project and each person will have a job."

2. Distribute Materials
Give each team one plate, one large bag, several cups of sand, several cups of soil, and a variety of seeds (including the bean soup mix).

3. Pour Sand
"Student #1, your job will be to place the bag on the plate and open it wide. Then pour a half-inch layer of sand in the bottom of the bag."

4. Spread Soil
"Student #2, spread an inch of potting soil on top of the sand. Smooth it evenly across the sand."

5. Plant Seeds
"Student #3, choose at least 10 different kinds of seeds to plant and plant several of each kind. Spread them evenly across the top of the soil and add another thin layer of soil to cover the seeds."

6. Water Seeds
"Student #4, sprinkle several tablespoons of water across the soil surface. The soil should be very moist but not muddy."

7. Record Observations
Give one copy of the Rain Forest in a Bag Observation Log to Student #1. "Everyone discuss what should be written beside Day 1 on your Observation Log. Student #1 will record your ideas today. You

Cooperative Structures
- Team Project
- Think-Pair-Share

Content Area
- Science

Materials
- Gallon-sized Ziploc bags (1 per team)
- Sturdy trays or paper plates (1 per team)
- Sand or gravel (Small bag for the class)
- Potting soil (Large bag for the class)
- 15 Bean soup mix (1 bag for the class)
- A variety of other seeds (grass, corn, squash, etc.)
- Rain Forest in a Bag Observation Log (1 per team)

Multiple Intelligences
- Verbal/Linguistic
- Visual/Spatial
- Bodily/Kinesthetic
- Naturalist
- Interpersonal

Rain Forest in a Bag

will rotate the role of Recorder each day." Collect the logs or store them in a safe place. Place the bags in a warm location.

Caution: When moving the bags, pick up the entire plate very carefully. Jarring the bag will cause the root systems to become damaged.

8. Discuss Transpiration

After the plants have grown several inches, zip the bag closed and leave in the sun for several hours. Ask students to observe the moisture that collects on the insides of the bag. Then Think-Pair-Share the question, *"Where is the moisture coming from?"* Explain that some of the moisture is given off by the leaves in a process called transpiration. An enormous amount of moisture is released by the trees of the rain forest. In fact, scientists say the rain forest creates its own weather due to transpiration. Cutting down the trees changes the climate drastically. (Be sure to open the rain forest bags after this part of the activity.)

9. Discuss Biodiversity

Tell students that you had them plant a large variety of seeds to demonstrate the concept of **biodiversity.** Allow teams to look up the word parts "bio" and "diversity" and to discuss the possible meanings of biodiversity. Explain that the rain forest has a greater variety of living things per square mile than any other place on earth. When people cut down rain forests they are destroying thousands of different plant and animal species.

Journal Idea

After the investigation is over, ask students to summarize what they learned about transpiration and biodiversity.

Rain Forest in a Bag Observation Log

Team Name _____

Date	Observations

Vivid Vocabulary

Students learn a dozen colorful words and use them to color a butterfly and write a descriptive paragraph.

ACTIVITY 16

Steps...

Cooperative Structures
- Jigsaw
- RoundRobin

Content Areas
- Reading
- Language Arts
- Art

Materials
- **Colors** worksheets 1 - 4 (1 set per team)
- **Colorful Butterfly** worksheet (1 per person)
- Crayons, markers, glitter pens, etc.
- Dictionaries (1 per person or team)

Literature Links
One Day in the Tropical Rain Forest by Jean Craighead George

Multiple Intelligences
- Verbal/Linguistic
- Visual/Spatial
- Naturalist
- Interpersonal

1. Introduce Activity
"In a few days I will read you a story called **One Day in the Tropical Rain Forest.** As I read, you'll discover that plants and animals of the rain forest often have very brilliant and unusual coloration. Today you will learn about some of the color words you'll hear later in the story."

2. Assign Roles
"Each of you will become an 'expert' on just three colors. Number off from 1 to 4 in your teams." Give each team one set of four Colors worksheets. Have students distribute them to team members according to the number in the upper right corner.

3. Form Expert Groups
Students who have the same number meet together in a corner of the room. Designate each meeting place by number. "Take a dictionary and move to your Expert Groups. Together look up each word and write its color-related definition. Then illustrate each color or find an example to show its meaning." (Students may think of using such items as plastic wrap, a coin, or aluminum foil.)

4. Reunite and Teach
"Now return to your original teams. Take turns teaching your teammates about your three color words. Start with Student #1."

5. Color Butterflies
Give each person one Butterfly worksheet and coloring materials. "As you color your butterfly, think of the color words you learned. Later you will use those words to describe your butterfly."

6. Write Descriptions
When students are done coloring, have them describe

Activity 16 continued
Vivid Vocabulary

Variation
- **Note-taking** – During step 4 have students take notes during the sharing section. Ask them to list all 12 words in their journals and write a synonym or brief description of each color word.

Journal Idea
Let students draw and color a different rain forest plant or animal in their journals. Then have them write a brief description under the picture using as many color words as possible.

their butterflies. *"Now write a description of your butterfly using as many of the vivid vocabulary words as possible. Check off each word as you use it. Don't worry if you can't use them all."*

7. RoundRobin
After everyone finishes, have them RoundRobin read their butterfly descriptions to their teams. For an extra challenge, have them separate the pictures from the descriptions. Place the pictures in the center of the team and ask team members to identify each picture as its description is read.

Colors #1

scarlet

Definition:
_____
_____
_____
_____

Example

iridescent

Definition:
_____
_____
_____
_____

Example

vivid

Definition:
_____
_____
_____
_____

Example

Colors #2

crimson

Definition:
_____
_____
_____
_____

Example

checkered

Definition:
_____
_____
_____
_____

Example

metallic

Definition:
_____
_____
_____
_____

Example

Colors #3

multi-colored

Definition:
_____
_____
_____
_____
_____

Example

copper

Definition:
_____
_____
_____
_____
_____

Example

tangerine

Definition:
_____
_____
_____
_____
_____

Example

Colors #4

violet

Definition:
_____
_____
_____
_____

Example

transparent

Definition:
_____
_____
_____
_____

Example

silver

Definition:
_____
_____
_____
_____

Example

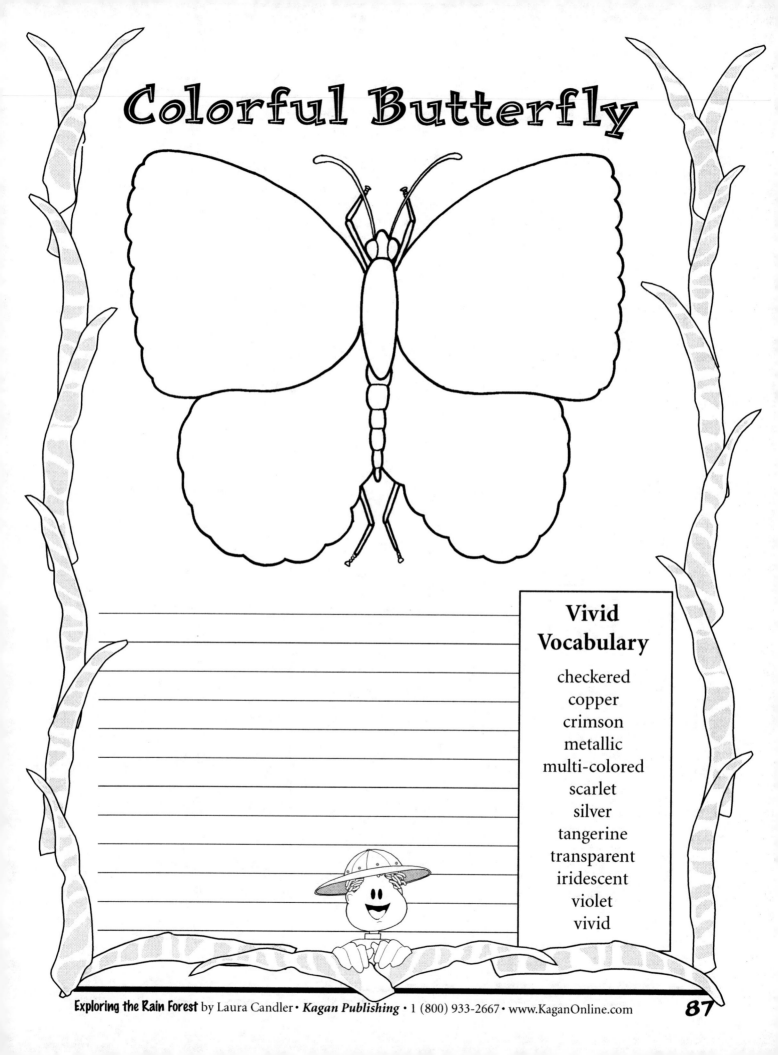

It's About Time

Students construct clocks and review telling time with an analog clock face. Then students set their clocks to specific times as they listen to the book, One Day in the Tropical Rain Forest.

ACTIVITY 17

Cooperative Structures
- **Numbered Heads Together**
- **RoundTable**
- **Team Project**

Content Areas
- Mathematics
- Reading

Materials
- 9" diameter paper plates (1 per team)
- **Clock Pattern** (1 per team)
- Paper fasteners (1 per team)
- Scissors (1 per team)
- Glue (1 bottle per team)
- Hole puncher (at least 1 per class)

Literature Links
One Day in the Tropical Rain Forest by Jean Craighead George

Multiple Intelligences
- **Verbal/Linguistic**
- **Logical/Mathematical**
- **Visual/Spatial**
- **Naturalist**
- **Interpersonal**

Steps...

1. Introduce Activity
Duplicate the Clock Pattern on white construction paper or card stock if possible. Give each team one set of materials for making a clock. *"Today your team will make a clock face from a paper plate. Each of you will be assigned a job. Number off from 1 to 4 in your teams and then I will explain your roles."*

2. Assign Roles
As you name and describe each role, list the student number and job on the board for reference. *"Student #1 cuts out the clock face and colors the hands of the clock. Color the hour hand red and the minute hand blue. Student #2 cuts out the hands of the clock and punches a hole at the end of each hand. Student #3 uses the paper fastener to attach the hands to the middle. Student #4 glues the clock to the paper plate, making sure the hands can turn freely."*

3. Construct Clocks
Give students about 10 minutes to construct their clocks according to the directions listed on the board. Monitor and assist where needed.

4. Numbered Heads Practice
After teams have constructed their clocks, use Numbered Heads Together to review their time skills. Call out a time such as "2:45" and have students put their heads together to discuss, *without actually moving the hands,* how they would set the clock. Randomly call out a number from 1 to 4. The person on each team having that number sets the clock face correctly (without team help). All students whose number is called hold up their clocks for you to check. Repeat several times for practice.

ACTIVITY 17 continued
It's About Time

Variation
- **Showdown** – If you prefer to have each child make his or her own clock, prepare enough materials and have each child follow the basic directions. Use only one team clock for step 4 but return all clocks to students for step 5. Each time you call out a new time in the story, have the students follow the Showdown directions (page 176).

Journal Idea
After completing the story (which may take several read aloud sessions), have students think of the important events in their school day. Ask them to draw at least 5 clock faces showing those times. Have them write a sentence next to each clock face explaining the important event.

5. Read Aloud/Set Clocks
Read aloud *One Day in the Tropical Rain Forest*. This is the story of a day in the life of Tepui, a rain forest native who is trying to find a new species of butterfly. The story gives exact times of important events throughout the Tepui's day. Before you begin say, *"As I read, you and your teammates will take turns setting the hands on the clock to match the time of each event in the story. Student #2 will set the first time when I read it aloud. After holding up the clock to be checked by the team, he or she passes the clock to Student #3. As soon as I announce the time of the next event, that person will change the clock to show the new time. Continue setting the new time and passing the clock throughout the story."*

Same-Different

In pairs, students compare two similar pictures of the rain forest to discover what's the same and what's different. The catch... they can't see each other's picture!

ACTIVITY 18

Cooperative Structure
- Same-Different

Content Areas
- Science
- Art

Materials
- **Tropical Rain Forest Picture 1** and **Picture 2** (1 set per pair)
- **Same-Different Recording Sheet** (1 per person)
- File folders (2 per pair)
- Paper clips (1 per pair)

Multiple Intelligences
- Verbal/Linguistic
- Logical/Mathematical
- Visual/Spatial
- Naturalist
- Interpersonal

Steps...

1. Prepare Materials

Duplicate Picture 1 and Picture 2 on two different colors of paper if possible. This will enable you to keep track at a glance of who has what picture.

2. Distribute Materials

Divide students into pairs and give each pair two file folders and one paper clip. Seat partners facing each other. Show them how to set up a barrier between them using open file folders and a paper clip (refer to illustration, page 176). Give each pair both pictures and two Recording Sheets. Distribute the pictures face down, using the colored paper to guide you. When each person has a picture, have them turn the pictures face up.

3. Model Activity

Stand next to a pair of students as you model the activity. "Tonya and Joe have slightly different pictures of the rain forest. Their job is to discover how the pictures are alike and different without actually looking at each others' pictures. There are at least 20 things that are the same and 20 that are different. They will record how the pictures are different and alike on their Venn diagrams. For example, Tonya might ask, 'Do you have a boa constrictor on a tree trunk?' If Joe's picture does not have a boa on a tree, they would record the information in the outer portion of the Picture 1 circle. If Joe's picture does have a snake on a tree, that detail would be recorded in the overlapping area since it is the same in both pictures. They will take turns asking questions until they find all 20 differences."

4. Same-Different

Give students time to play Same-Different. Then say, "When you are done, take down your barriers and compare pictures and Venn Diagrams. Discuss the differences you found and see if you can find any more."

Exploring the Rain Forest by Laura Candler • Kagan Publishing • 1 (800) 933-2667 • www.KaganOnline.com

Picture 1
Tropical Rain Forest

Picture 2
Tropical Rain Forest

Same-Different Recording Sheet

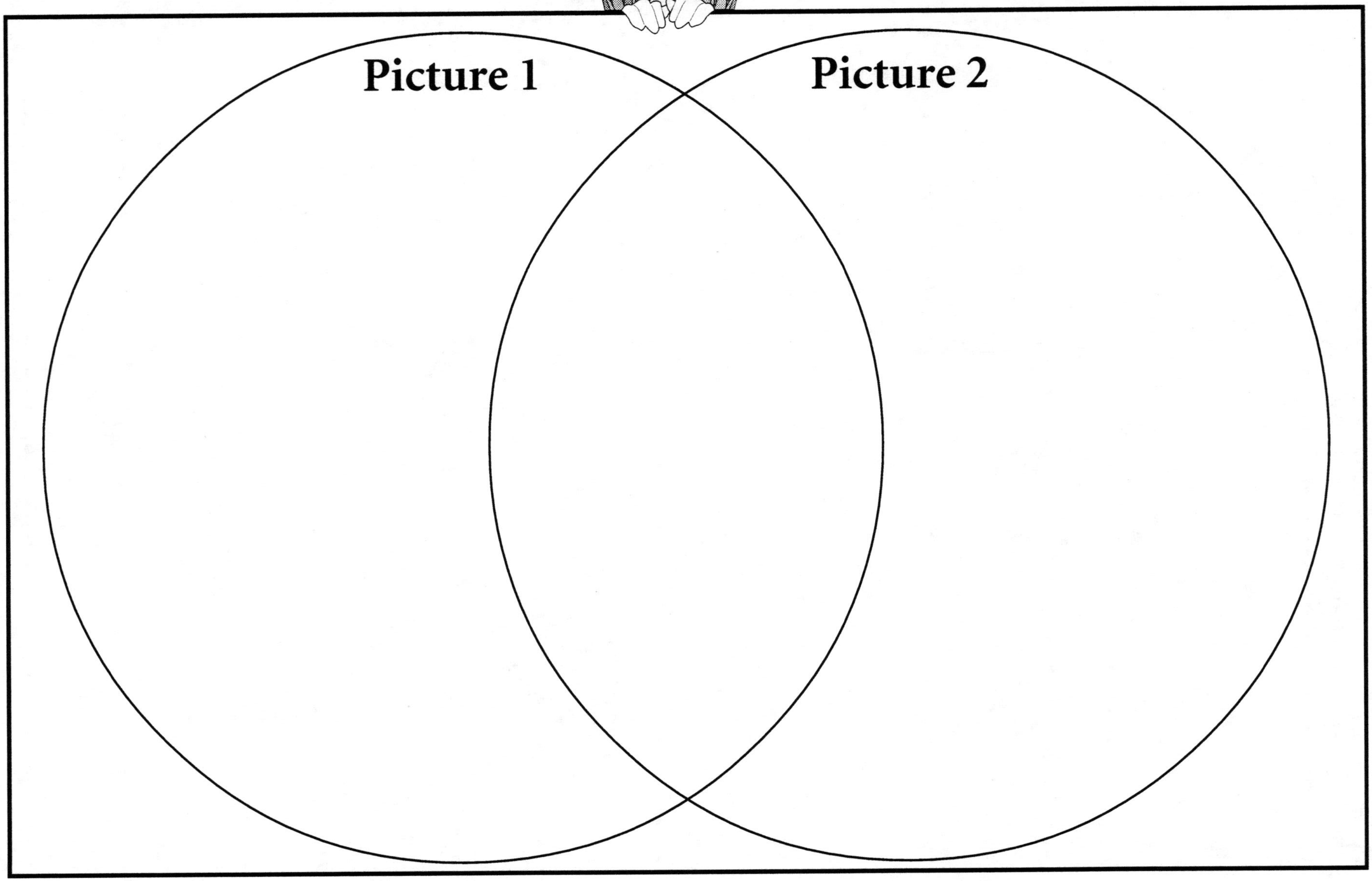

Picture 1

Picture 2

96 Exploring the Rain Forest by Laura Candler • Kagan Publishing • 1 (800) 933-2667 • www.KaganOnline.com

Jigsaw Story Mapping

Students listen to a rain forest story. They break into groups to discuss the parts of the story, then return to their teams to share what they learned.

ACTIVITY 19

Steps...

1. Review Story Elements

Choose the story map you will use for this activity. Explain the parts of a story using a literature selection familiar to your students.

2. Read Aloud

"Now that you know the parts of a story, listen to this story about the rain forest. As I read, think about the parts of the story. Be prepared to discuss them later." Read aloud *The Great Kapok Tree* or another fictional piece with a clear plot.

3. Introduce Jigsaw

Divide students into teams of four if you are using Story Map A or teams of three if you are using Story Map B. (The following directions assume the use of Map A. Modify accordingly if you are using Map B.) Distribute the Story Maps and assign students in each team a number from 1 to 4. "Within your teams you are going to map out the events of the story. Each of you is responsible for one part of the story map. The students assigned #1 will meet to discuss the beginning. All #2's will meet to discuss the middle, the #3's will talk about the climax, and the #4's will discuss the conclusion. "Have students move to one of the four stations set up before hand."

4. Expert Groups Meet

Meet with each group briefly to make sure they can describe their part of the book you read aloud. Have them write a brief description on the lines of their story map.

5. Teams Reunite and Share

"Now return to your original teams. Student #1 will describe the events of the story's beginning. Without copying, each of you will write the beginning on your own worksheets in your own words. Next, Student #2 describes the middle, #3

Cooperative Structures
- Jigsaw
- RoundRobin

Content Areas
- Reading
- Language Arts

Materials
- Story Map A or B (1 per person)

Literature Links
The Great Kapok Tree, One Day in the Tropical Rain Forest, Save My Rainforest, or other rain forest fiction with a clear plot

Multiple Intelligences
- **Verbal/Linguistic**
- **Logical/Mathematical**
- **Visual/Spatial**
- **Naturalist**
- **Interpersonal**

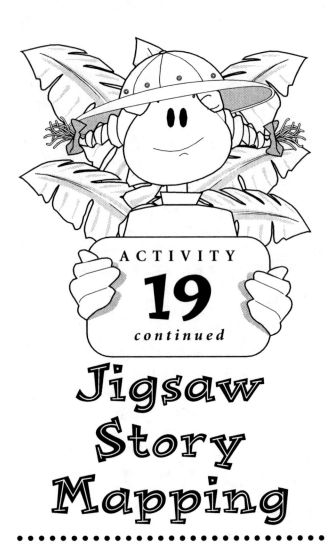

Jigsaw Story Mapping

explains the climax, and #4 tells about the conclusion. When you are finished, each of you will have a complete story map."

Journal Idea

In their journals, have students write a brief summary of the story you read aloud. Ask them to give their opinion of the story, explaining why they liked it or did not like it.

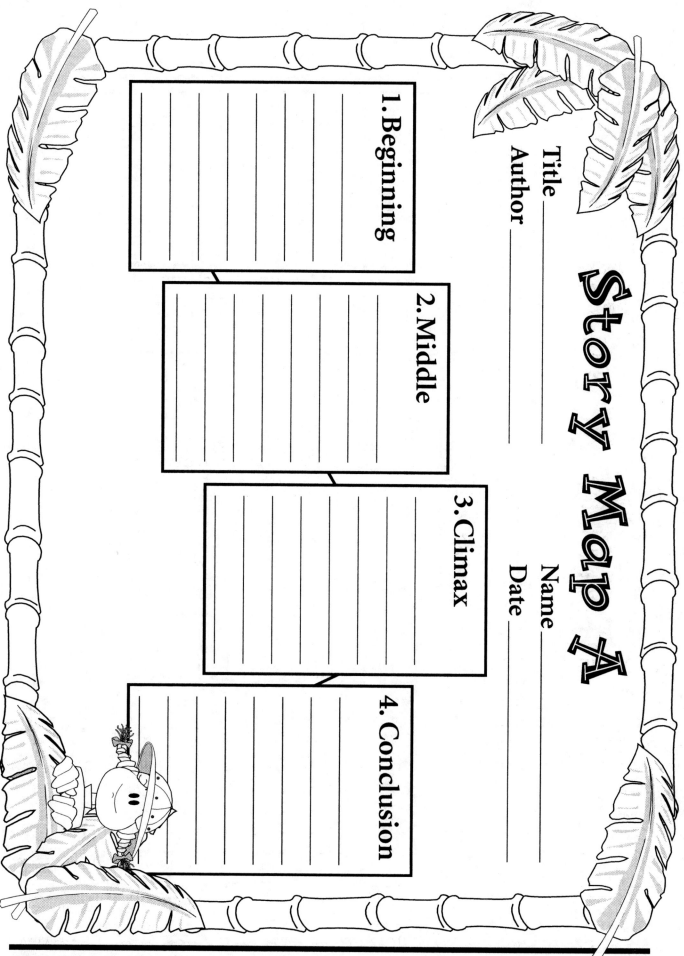

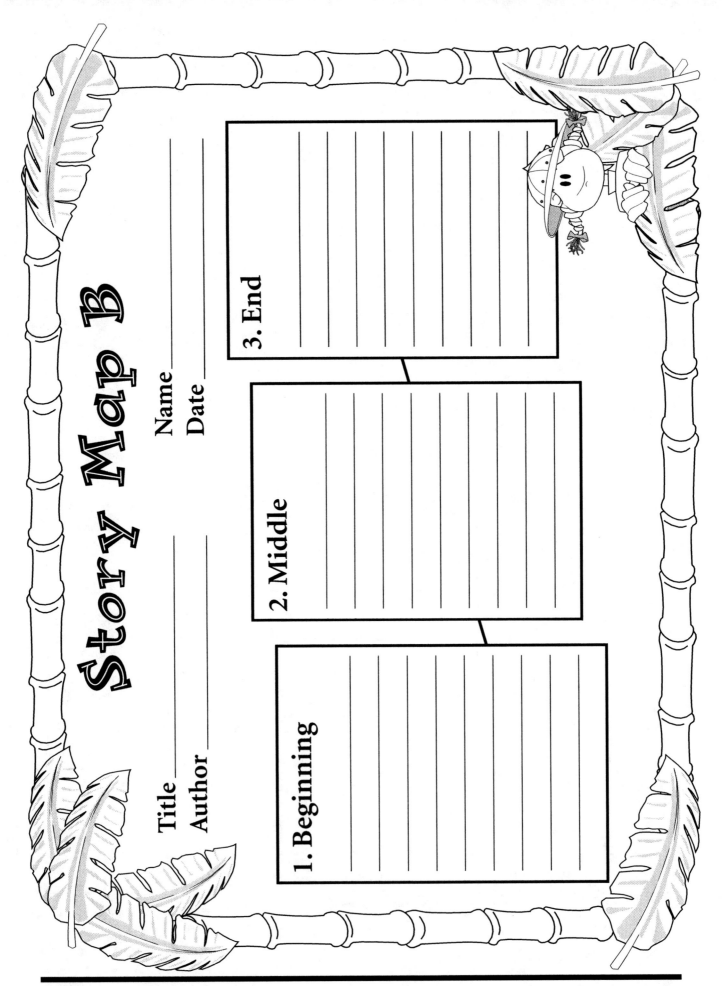

Comparing Kids

Students listen to a story about a real boy named Antonio who lives in a rain forest. They compare Antonio's life to their own.

ACTIVITY 20

Steps...

Cooperative Structures
- Pairs Compare
- RallyRobin
- RallyTable

Content Areas
- Science
- Social Studies
- Reading
- Language Arts

Materials
- **Comparing Kids Graphic Organizer** (1 per pair)
- Colored pencils (2 different colors per pair)

Literature Links
Antonio's Rain Forest by Anna Lewington

Multiple Intelligences
- Verbal/Linguistic
- Logical/Mathematical
- Visual/Spatial
- Naturalist
- Interpersonal

1. RallyRobin

"Today I'm going to read you a true story about a boy named Antonio who lives in the rain forest. Before I read, I want you to think about how his life might be different from yours." After 10 - 15 seconds think time, say "Now turn to your partner and talk about your ideas. Take turns naming ways that you think Antonio's life might be different from yours."

2. Read Aloud

Read aloud *Antonio's Rain Forest*. As you read, be sure to show your class the photographs and illustrations which graphically portray this boy's story.

3. Complete Graphic Organizers

Give each pair one graphic organizer and two different colored pencils for accountability. Have them complete the worksheet in RallyTable fashion. *"Each of you choose a color and write your name on your paper now."* Pause. *"You and your partner will talk about how your life is like Antonio's and how it's different. As you think of ideas, take turns writing them in the correct space on the graphic organizer. If something is true about your life, write it in the top left box. If it's true about Antonio's life, record it in the top right box. If the statement is true about both, write that idea in the bottom box. Try to see how many ideas you can come up within five minutes."*

4. Pairs Compare

After 5 minutes, say *"Stop. Compare your graphic organizers with the one your teammates completed. Take turns checking off the items that you both have, and write in anything that you are missing. When you finish, both graphic organizers should have the same ideas."*

Exploring the Rain Forest by Laura Candler • **Kagan Publishing** • 1 (800) 933-2667 • www.KaganOnline.com

ACTIVITY 20 continued

Comparing Kids

5. Team Challenge

"Now within your team of four, see if you can add any more details. Take turns adding them to your own graphic organizers."

Journal Idea

Following this activity, have students write a paragraph in their journals comparing their life to Antonio's. Then suggest that they write a story in which Antonio comes for a visit.

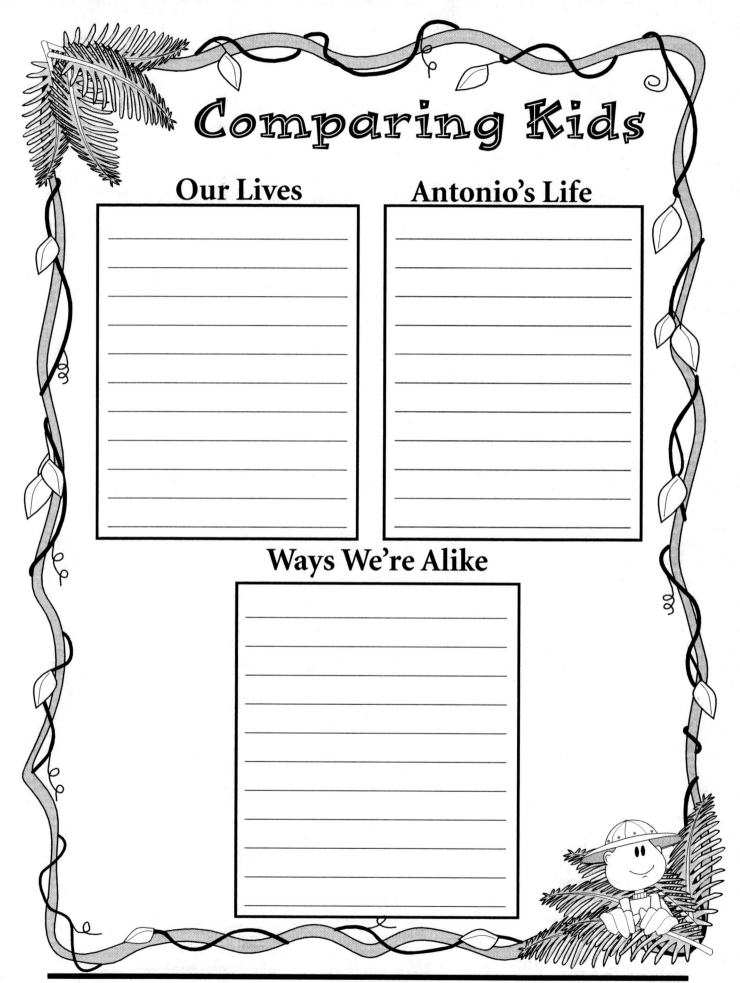

Erosion Experiment

Through experimentation, students discover the importance of plant roots in preventing soil erosion.

ACTIVITY 21

Cooperative Structure
- Team Project

Content Area
- Science

Materials
- Erosion Experiment Lab Report (1 per person)
- Trays or cookie sheets (2 per team)
- Potting soil (1 large bag for the class)
- Grass seed (1/4 cup per team)
- Watering can with a sprinkler top (1 per class)

Multiple Intelligences
- Verbal/Linguistic
- Logical/Mathematical
- Visual/Spatial
- Bodily/Kinesthetic
- Naturalist
- Interpersonal

Steps...

1. Discuss Erosion
Give each person one Lab Report. Divide each team into pairs and ask them, *"What is soil erosion? What effects do plants have on soil erosion?"* Have them turn to their partner and discuss their ideas. Ask them to use their ideas to write a hypothesis on their lab report.

2. Prepare Trays
Give each team two trays, several cups of potting soil, and 1/4 cup of grass seed. Ask them to follow the steps 1 - 4 of the procedure carefully. Place the trays in a warm sunny place where students can observe their progress. Water just enough to keep the soil moist. Allow the grass to grow at least a week before continuing with the experiment.

3. Water Trays
When the grass has had time to develop a root system, have each team take their trays outside for the experiment. One at a time, allow each group to come forward for the demonstration. Tilt both trays at about a 30° angle to represent a hillside. Sprinkle water from the watering can over each tray. Observe the effects of plant roots on soil erosion.

4. Write Results
Say, *"Complete the Results section of your lab report by writing a description of what you observed. You may discuss your ideas with your team before you begin writing, but end the discussion before you pick up your pencil to write."* Allow time for completing the Results portion of the lab report.

5. Write Conclusion
"Now, with your team, talk over the reason why the soil in the grassy tray did not erode when you watered it. This statement explaining your results is called your Conclusion. Once again, you may discuss your ideas with your team but write your own conclusions on the lab report."

Erosion Experiment

Journal Idea

Explain the "slash and burn" method of clearing rain forest land to your class. Ask students to write about the effects of this on a region that receives as much as 200 or 300 inches of rain a year.

Erosion Experiment Lab Report

Question
Name _____

What effect will plant roots have on soil erosion?

Hypothesis
_____
_____

Materials
- 2 trays
- potting soil
- grass seed
- watering can

Procedure
1. Divide the potting soil evenly between the two trays, saving about 1/2 cup for later.
2. Spread the soil completely over each tray, pressing it lightly in place.
3. Sprinkle the grass seed over one of the trays, then sprinkle the remaining soil over the seeds.
4. Water both trays just enough to make the soil moist, not muddy.
5. After the grass grows for at least a week, tilt both trays at a 30° angle. Then use the watering can to "rain" on both trays. Observe.

Results
_____
_____
_____
_____

Conclusion
_____
_____
_____
_____

Words in a Word

Students work in pairs to make words using the letters in "Tropical Rain Forest."

ACTIVITY 22

Cooperative Structures
- RallyTable
- Blackboard Share

Content Areas
- Reading
- Language Arts

Materials
- **Words in a Word** worksheet (1 per pair)
- Colored pencils (2 different colors per pair)
- Dictionaries (1 per pair)
- Scissors (at least 1 per pair)

Multiple Intelligences
- Verbal/Linguistic
- Visual/Spatial
- Bodily/Kinesthetic
- Naturalist
- Interpersonal

Steps...

1. Distribute Materials
Divide your class into pairs and give each pair one Words in a Word worksheet, scissors, and a dictionary. Have them cut apart the letters at the bottom of the page.

2. Model Activity
Stand beside one pair of students and use them to demonstrate as you describe the activity. "How many words do you think you can find using the letters in 'Tropical Rain Forest?' You and your partner will work together to make smaller words from these letters. One of you will move the letters around until you find a word. You may use your dictionaries to check the correct spellings. The other person records the word on the worksheet using his or her colored pencil. Then switch roles so that the other person moves the letters to make the next word. You must take turns throughout the activity, so I will see alternating colors on the worksheet. Be sure each word has at least three letters and do not use proper nouns of any kind."

3. List Words
Allow plenty of time for students to make words from the letters in "Tropical Rain Forest." Monitor to make sure they are taking turns in RallyTable fashion (look for alternating colors on the recorded answers.) Halfway through the activity, stop them and ask, "What is the longest word you can make from the letters? Be prepared to write it on the board at the end of the activity."

4. Share Longest Word
When the time is up, have one person from each pair come to the board and write the longest word they found.

Words in a Word

How many words can you find in the letters of "Tropical Rain Forest?" Cut out the letters below and use them to help you make words. Work with a partner and take turns finding words and writing them on the lines.

1. _____
2. _____
3. _____
4. _____
5. _____
6. _____
7. _____
8. _____
9. _____
10. _____
11. _____
12. _____
13. _____
14. _____
15. _____
16. _____
17. _____
18. _____
19. _____
20. _____
21. _____
22. _____
23. _____
24. _____
25. _____
26. _____
27. _____
28. _____
29. _____
30. _____
31. _____
32. _____
33. _____
34. _____
35. _____
36. _____
37. _____
38. _____
39. _____

T	R	O	P	I	C
A	L	R	A	I	N
F	O	R	E	S	T

Traveling Showdown

In teams, students solve math word problems. Then one team member "travels" to the next team to share and discuss the answer.

ACTIVITY 23

Steps...

1. Showdown

Number students off within teams from 1 to 4. Place the word problem transparency on the overhead. Read the first problem aloud to the class and say, *"Think of a strategy you can use to solve this problem. Use your calculator or paper and pencil to solve the problem and write down your answer."* Allow time for problem solving, then say *"It's time for a Showdown! Show your teammates your answers and discuss your solutions. Make sure everyone knows how to solve the problem correctly."*

2. Teammates Travel

Choose a number from 1 to 4 by spinning a spinner or rolling a die. Ask the student on each team with that number to stand. *"Move one team to your left. Tell your new team the answer to the problem and explain how your old team arrived at that answer."* Remind students to praise each other for correct solutions.

3. Discuss Solutions

Call on one team to share the answer with the class. Ask other students to share a variety of strategies for solving the problem.

4. Repeat

Uncover the next problem on the overhead and follow steps 2 - 4. To add in a "classbuilding" component, vary the number of teams and/or direction each person moves in the "traveling" step. For example, Student #1 might move 2 teams to the left, Student #2 might move 1 team to the right, and so on. By doing this, class members will be completely mixed at the end of the activity.

Cooperative Structure
- **Showdown**

Content Area
- Mathematics

Materials
- Transparency of **Rain Forest Word Problems** (Level A or B)
- Calculators (1 per person)
- Paper and pencil
- Randomizing device (student spinner or dice)

Multiple Intelligences
- **Verbal/Linguistic**
- **Logical/Mathematical**
- **Bodily/Kinesthetic**
- **Naturalist**
- **Interpersonal**

Rain Forest Word Problems
(Level A)

1. Scientists counted 23 new species of butterflies, 8 new bird species, and 16 new mammal species in the rain forest. How many new species is this in all?

2. If a toucan eats 3 pieces of fruit in one hour, how many pieces can it eat in 6 hours?

3. The temperature in one rain forest was 73° in the morning and 82° by afternoon. How much did the temperature increase during this time?

4. The same amount of rain fell each day for one week. If 14 inches of rain fell in that week, how many inches fell each day?

5. A sloth hangs 20 feet above the ground in a cacao tree. If she climbs down at a speed of 4 feet per minute, how many minutes will it take her to reach the ground?

Rain Forest Word Problems
(Level B)

1. Brazil's Amazon Rain Forest is the world's largest, covering about 2 million square miles. By comparison, only 4,000 square miles can be found in Australia. How many more miles of rain forest are in Brazil?

2. Many tropical rain forests receive an average of 25 inches of rain a month. Compare this to San Francisco, which receives only 20 inches *per year*. How much more does the average tropical rain forest receive than San Francisco in one year?

3. Scientists estimate that deforestation destroys an average of 2 plant or animal species per hour. At this rate, how many species become extinct in one year?

Rain Forest Word Problems
(Level B, continued)

4. Many rain forests are being destroyed to make land for cattle ranches. Over 120 million pounds of beef are imported by the U.S. each year. How many quarter pound hamburgers would that make? If each one sold for $2, how much money would Americans spend on rain forest beef in all?

5. A sloth, a monkey, a snake, and a frog were climbing up a kapok tree. They were arranged in a column, with the sloth just above the frog. The snake was not at the bottom, and the frog was between the monkey and the sloth. In what order were the animals on the tree?

Amazing Animals

In pairs, students research and illustrate a rain forest animal. They present their report to the class and place the animal on a large class kapok tree.

ACTIVITY 24

Steps...

1. Read Aloud
Read aloud *The Great Kapok Tree*. Ask students to listen and try to remember the different tropical animals named in the story. Show them the inside cover of the book which has detailed drawings of additional rain forest animals. Tell them that they will be learning more about the amazing animals that live in the rain forest.

2. Assign Animals
Cut apart the Amazing Animal Pictures. Divide students into pairs. If you have more than 24 students, form a few groups of three or choose additional animals not pictured. Give each pair one animal picture and one Amazing Animal Report form. Have them glue the picture in the box and write the animal's name on the line.

3. Research Animals
"*Together you and your partner will research your assigned animal. As you find the information needed, take turns writing it on the report form. Be sure to write in complete sentences.*"

4. Illustrate Animals
After students have completed their research say, "*Now work with your partner to create a picture of your animal using the art materials provided. You may draw and color it, or use construction paper to cut out the parts and glue it together. Use the animal's true colors and try to make your pictures as accurate as possible.*"

5. Present Reports
When every pair is ready say, "*You and your partner will come forward and tape your animal onto the kapok tree. One person will tell us about*

Cooperative Structure
- Pair Project

Content Areas
- Science
- Reading
- Language Arts
- Art

Materials
- **Amazing Animal Pictures** (1 or 2 copies per class)
- **Amazing Animal Report** form (1 per pair)
- Construction paper, scissors, crayons, and glue
- Tape
- Large drawing or cut-out of kapok tree

Literature Links
The Great Kapok Tree by Lynn Cherry

Multiple Intelligences
- Verbal/Linguistic
- Visual/Spatial
- Bodily/Kinesthetic
- Naturalist
- Interpersonal

Journal Idea

Challenge students to write a story about a day in the life of their animal. They should include details such as predators, foods, adaptations, etc.

Amazing Animals

the animal's food and enemies. The other person will tell how the animal survives and any other interesting facts. You will have two minutes to present your report. Do not read directly from your paper!"

Extension Activity

- **Internet Research** - *Students may enjoy visiting the "Animals in the Rainforest" Web site found at* http://www.geocities.com/Rainforest/5798/ani.html. *Here they can view photographs of selected animals. Clicking on a photograph will take them to a Web page with information about that animal.*

Amazing Animal Pictures-Set 1

Amazing Animal Pictures-Set 2

Agouti	Hawk	Python
Chameleon	Spider Monkey	Flying Fox
Kinkajou	Leaf Cutter Ant	Macaw
Praying Mantis	Hercules Beetle	Tree Porcupine

Amazing Animal Report

Name(s) _____

Animal _____

Rain Forest Layer _____

Food
_____
_____
_____

Enemies
_____
_____
_____

How It Survives
_____
_____
_____

Other Interesting Facts
_____
_____
_____

Mystery Animal

Each student secretly chooses a different mystery animal. Teammates try to guess each others' animals by asking yes/no questions.

ACTIVITY 25

Cooperative Structures
- Team Discussion
- Team Interview

Content Areas
- Science
- Language Arts

Materials
- **Amazing Animal Pictures** (1 set of 24 pictures per team - see pages 117-118)
- Scissors

Multiple Intelligences
- Verbal/Linguistic
- Logical/Mathematical
- Naturalist
- Interpersonal
- Bodily/Kinesthetic
- Intrapersonal

Steps...

1. Review
This activity works best after students have completed the Amazing Animals activity. Some prior knowledge of rain forest animals is necessary for students to experience success. Review the characteristics of the following animal classifications: insects, birds, mammals, reptiles, and amphibians.

2. Team Discussion
Give each team one sheet of Amazing Animals Pictures and number students off from 1 to 4 in their teams. Say, *"Cut apart the pictures, place them face up in the middle of the team, and discuss the animals with your teammates. What do you know about each animal? If no one on the team is familiar with an animal, remove it from the pile."*

3. Model Activity
"Now, we are going to play a guessing game called 'Mystery Animal.' I'm going to teach the game to you by playing against the class. I'm thinking of a Mystery Animal, and it's one of the 24 animals in front of you. I want you to take turns asking me yes/no questions to find out what the animal is. When your whole team thinks they know, Student #1 will write the team guess on a slip of paper." Encourage students to ask questions such as the ones shown in the sidebar. Play until at least half the teams know the animal. Applaud the teams that correctly guess your mystery animal.

Sample Questions
1. Is your animal a mammal?
2. Does it have a tail?
3. Is it colorful?
4. Does your animal have four legs?
5. Can your animal fly?
6. Does your animal eat meat?

ACTIVITY 25 continued

Mystery Animal

4. Select Animals

"Now you will play Mystery Animal within your own teams. Each of you secretly select one animal without letting anyone on your team know what you have chosen. Write down the name of your Mystery Animal and hide the slip of paper in your desk."

5. Team Interview

"To begin, Student #1 stands up. Team members take turns asking that person questions until they all think they know the Mystery Animal. At this point, the team huddles and agrees upon **one and only one guess.** They say their guess together. If they are correct, Student #1 claps for them. If they are not correct, he or she reveals the true mystery animal. Then Student #1 sits down and the next team member stands to be interviewed." Monitor the classroom as students play Mystery Animal. Make sure team members only make one team guess each time about the identity of the mystery animal. If some teams finish early, let team members choose another animal and play a second round.

Hints and Variations

- **Time Limit** - If some teams get stuck trying to guess one Mystery Animal, implement a 2-minute time limit per animal.
- **Hide Animal Pictures** - To make the game more challenging, have students turn the pictures upside-down and choose an animal without looking.
- **Limit Guesses** - To encourage higher-level thinking and to discourage wild guessing, give each student 3 dried beans to use as counters. Each time a student asks a question, he or she must give a bean to the interviewee. When everyone is out of beans, the team must try to guess the animal. Students quickly learn to think about each question carefully to avoid wasting beans. Redistribute the beans before each round.
- **Partners** - Students enjoy playing this game two-on-two. Each team divides into two sets of pairs. One pair selects an animal, and the other two students take turns asking questions. They switch roles after the first round. After the second round, form new pairs. This variation is useful with students of low academic ability.
- **Animal Charades** - If team members have trouble guessing the identity of the Mystery Animal, allow students to provide further clues by silently pantomiming the animal's actions.

Journal Idea

Have students choose a Mystery Animal to describe in their journals. Ask them to write a paragraph in which they describe the animal's characteristics without identifying the animal itself. Then have students switch journals, read each other's entries, and try to guess the identity of their partner's Mystery Animal.

Food Chain Fun

Students assume the roles of rain forest plants and animals. They mix around the room, then form food chains by linking arms.

ACTIVITY 26

Cooperative Structures
- Mix-Freeze-Group
- Think-Pair-Share

Content Area
- Science

Materials
- **Food Chain Fun** pictures (1 set of 24 cards per class)
- 20" pieces of yarn (1 per person)
- Hole puncher
- Rain Forest music (optional)

Literature Links
Here Is the Tropical Rain Forest by Madeleine Dunphy

Multiple Intelligences
- Verbal/Linguistic
- Visual/Spatial
- Musical/Rhythmic
- Bodily/Kinesthetic
- Naturalist
- Interpersonal
- Intrapersonal

Steps...

1. Prepare Signs
Prepare the food chain signs for this activity in advance. Duplicate the 24 Food Chain Fun pictures on construction paper or card stock if possible. If you need additional pictures, make extra harpy eagles, jaguars, and boa constrictors since they can go at the end of any food chain. If you have two or more extra students, you can make an additional sun and a plant card. *Always make sure you have the same number of suns as plants.* Cut the pictures apart and punch two holes in the top of each card. String a piece of yarn through the two holes so that the card may be worn around the neck as a small sign.

2. Read Aloud
Read aloud *Here Is the Tropical Rain Forest* and ask students to notice the ways that the plants and animals in the story depend on each other.

3. Think-Pair-Share
Ask students to think, *"Where does the energy for all living things come from?"* After 10 or 15 seconds of think time, have them pair with a partner to discuss their ideas. Then call on someone to share with the class. Make sure they understand the food chain concept, including the idea that all living things directly or indirectly get their energy from the sun.

4. Model Activity
Give each student one food chain card. Have them wear the signs around their necks. Ask one person with a sun card to come forward. *"What living things in the rain forest get their energy directly from the sun?"* Call one person

Exploring the Rain Forest by Laura Candler • Kagan Publishing • 1 (800) 933-2667 • www.KaganOnline.com

Food Chain Fun

Activity 26 continued

with a plant card to come forward since plants always make up the next level of the food chain. Ask the plant to stand to the left of the sun so that the arrow is pointing up the food chain. *"The sun gives energy to the plant."* Ask someone with a bird card to step forward. Link the students and describe the new chain that is formed.

5. Review Animals

"Before we begin to make other food chains, we need to know what each animal eats." Ask the students wearing animal signs to stand one-by-one. As each person stands, quickly review what that animal eats. You may want to make a chart of this information to post on the board.

6. Mix-Freeze-Group

"Each of you is wearing a picture card showing one part of a rain forest food chain. When I say 'Mix' walk around the room until I ask you to freeze. Mix!" After a few moments say, *"Freeze! Now look at the people around you and try to make a food chain. You may have as many people as you want in your chain as long as it's scientifically correct. If you can't find anyone to chain with, come to the front of the room. Once a group has formed a food chain, link arms and move to the edges of the room."*

7. Check Food Chains

After all possible food chains have been formed, check to make sure they are correct.

8. Trade and Repeat

Ask students to trade signs with someone in the class. If anyone was not in a chain, give them a sun card so they will be sure to be a part of the next chain. Repeat the activity as time allows.

Hints and Variations

- **Color-Coded Cards** - To simplify the game, duplicate the suns on yellow paper, the plants on green, and the animals on blue or red. This color coding will allow students to form food chains more easily.
- **Silent Rounds** - After students are proficient at forming food chains, challenge them to do the activity in total silence.
- **Musical Rounds** – Play rain forest music during each round of Mix-Freeze-Group. Have students begin mixing when the music starts, and instruct them to freeze when you stop the music. Then follow the basic activity directions to form the food chains.

Journal Idea

Have students draw a food chain in their journals. Then ask, *"What would happen to the rain forest food chain if all the trees and plants were killed?"* Ask them to write a few sentences describing what effect this would have on the food chain they drew.

Food Chain Fun
Consumers

boa constrictor
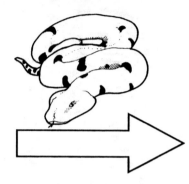
→

howler monkey

→

toucan

→

tree frog
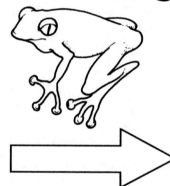
→

jaguar
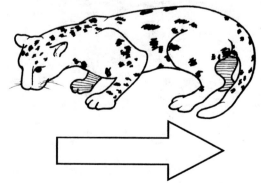
→

anteater
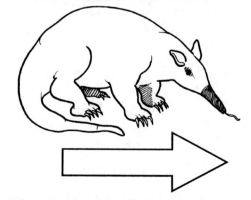
→

Food Chain Fun
Consumers

ant
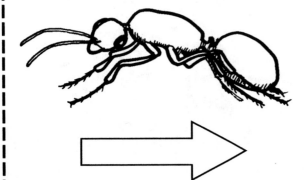

iguana
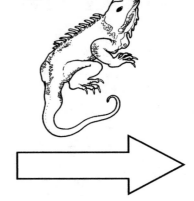

harpy eagle

termite
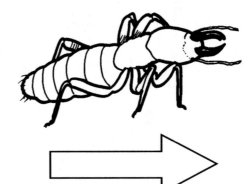

hummingbird

sloth
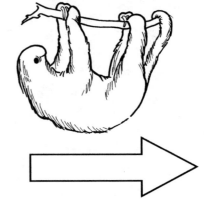

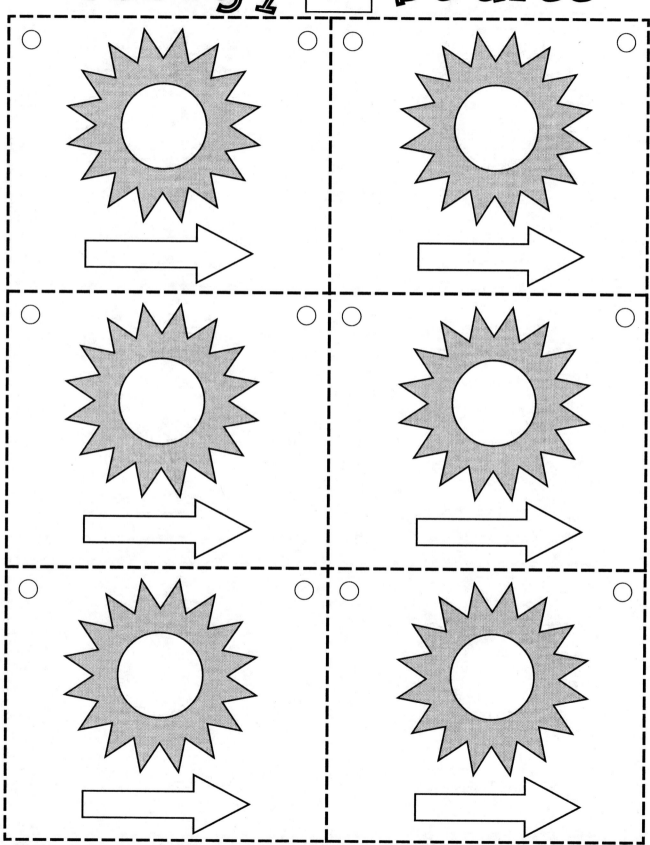

Food Chain Fun
Producers

Create a Creature

Students in teams invent an animal that is specially adapted to the rain forest environment. They create a tear-art picture of the creature and present it to the class.

ACTIVITY 27

Steps...

1. List Adaptations

"What adaptations, or special features, do animals have that help them to survive? For example, a porcupine's sharp quills protect it from its enemies. Student #1, write one animal and its adaptation on a sheet of paper. Then pass the paper to Student #2. Keep passing the paper and listing animals and adaptations until I call time."

2. Discuss Creatures

"Think about the special environment of the rain forest. It's a warm, wet jungle, filled with trees, vines, and living creatures. The Understory is damp and dark. The Canopy is warm and sunny. I want your team to invent an animal that could survive in the rain forest. Your animal must have at least four special features that help it survive in a tropical environment. Talk over your ideas, discussing colors and adaptations. Be sure to think of a name for your creature."

3. Create Creatures

When each team has thought of an animal, say, "Send one person to the materials table to get one sheet of white construction paper for the background and any other colors you need. For this activity, you may not use scissors, pencils, or markers. You may only tear the sheets of construction paper and glue them to create your animal. You may tear many small pieces and layer them, or tear out a smaller number of large pieces. Everyone must be actively working until the creature is finished."

4. Describe Adaptations

Give each team one Create a Creature worksheet and ask one person to write the creature's name at the top. "I want you to pass the worksheet around the team. Each person completes one part by describing one of your creature's adaptations."

Cooperative Structures
- RoundTable
- Team Project

Content Areas
- Science
- Language Arts
- Art

Materials
- Create a Creature worksheet (1 per team)
- 12" x 18" sheets of white construction paper (1 per team)
- Colored construction paper
- Glue
- Paper and pencil

Multiple Intelligences
- Verbal/Linguistic
- Visual/Spatial
- Naturalist
- Interpersonal
- Intrapersonal

Create a Creature

5. Present Creatures

Let each team come forward and show their creature. Ask each member of the team to explain one of its special features. Post the creatures and descriptions for everyone to view.

Journal Idea

In their journals, have each student draw a picture of their team creature. Ask them to write a brief description of the animal under the picture.

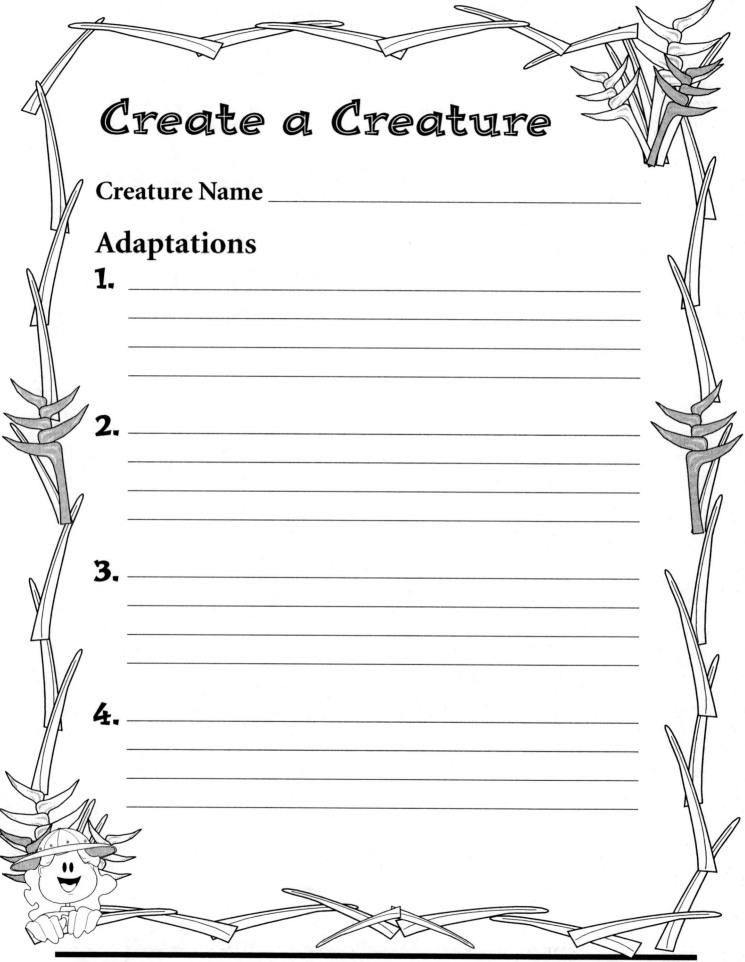

Create a Creature

Creature Name _____

Adaptations

1. _____

2. _____

3. _____

4. _____

Write Around

ACTIVITY 28

Students write team stories by adding several sentences to each story before passing it to the next person. They choose a favorite team story and present it to the class.

Steps...

Cooperative Structures
- RoundRobin
- RoundTable
- Spend-A-Buck

Content Area
- Language Arts
- Music

Materials
- **Story Starters** (4 different stories - 1 set per team)
- Colored pencils - 4 different dark colors per team
- Rain forest music or sounds
- **Rain Forest Bucks** (5 bucks per person, use blacklines in Activity 35)

Multiple Intelligences
- Verbal/Linguistic
- Musical/Rhythmic
- Naturalist
- Interpersonal

1. Introduce Activity

Give each team a set of 4 Story Starters and 4 colored pencils. Have them place the pages face down in the center of the team and take turns selecting a paper and a colored pencil. *"Today you will write team stories using these story starters. Everyone will begin writing on the Story Starter they chose. I will turn on the music and play it while you write. Use the colored pencil and write until you hear the music stop."*

2. Write Stories

Turn on the music and allow several minutes for students to begin their stories. After they have written several sentences, stop the music. *"Now pass your papers to the right. Keep the same color pencil. Silently read the new story starter and what your teammate has already written. Add to the story."* Continue to stop and start the music, having students pass papers in RoundTable fashion as you do so. After the third writing session, tell students to pass their papers one final time and add an ending to the story they receive.

3. Read Stories

In RoundRobin fashion, have students take turns reading aloud the story they just completed. *"Student #4 will read his or her story to the team. Then Students #1, #2, and #3 will read also. As each person reads, listen carefully. In a few minutes you will have to choose your favorite team story."*

4. Choose Favorite Story

Have teams use Spend-A-Buck to choose their favorite story. Give each person five paper bucks. *"Place all stories side by side in the middle of the team. Vote for your favorite stories by placing paper bucks on them. You may place all five bucks on one story or several bucks on several stories. After everyone has spent their bucks, count them to find the winning story."*

Activity 28 continued: Write Around

5. Practice Presentations
"Practice reading the winning story aloud. Pass the paper to the person who started the story. After they read their part, they pass it to the next person. Use the color coding to help you remember who wrote what."

6. Present Team Stories
Call on one team at a time to present their favorite story to the class. As each team comes forward, have them stand in the order in which they wrote the story. In RoundRobin fashion, each person reads his or her own part to the class.

Story Starter 1

The little green tree frog peered up to the top of the kapok tree towering above him. He had spent his entire life on the forest floor and wondered what it would be like to climb to the top of the great tree...

Story Starter 2

The jungle animals gathered in the rain forest for a council meeting. Their leader, a colorful toucan, announced that something had to be done to stop the cattle ranchers. They had just begun clearing land for a new ranch...

Story Starter 3

Daryl gripped the edges of his seat as the small plane took off. He had won a trip to the Amazon Rain Forest and today marked the beginning of his adventure...

Story Starter 4

As the sun rose, Sarana quietly slipped out of her village. Her grandmother was very sick, and Sarana had promised to find a cure for her illness. She needed just two petals from the magical rainbow flower that grew deep in the rain forest...

Math Talk

ACTIVITY 29

Students solve word problems by discussing strategies with teammates. Then each person individually writes the answer and an explanation of the problem-solving steps.

Steps...

Cooperative Structure
- **Teammates Consult**

Content Areas
- Mathematics
- Science

Materials
- **Math Talk** directions (1 transparency per class)
- **Rain Forest Word Problems** (1 worksheet per person)
- Large cup for pencils (1 per team)
- Calculators (1 per person)

Materials
- **Verbal/Linguistic**
- **Logical/Mathematical**

1. Distribute Materials
Place a large cup in the center of each team and give each person a Rain Forest Word Problems worksheet. Ask everyone to place their pencils in the cup. Number students off 1 to 4.

2. Model Activity
Put the Math Talk transparency on the overhead. Stand next to a team and say, *"Today you are going to work with your team to solve word problems. This activity is called 'Math Talk' because you will talk over your ideas for each problem before writing your own answer. Watch and listen as I have this team demonstrate the steps. Student #1 on this team will be the first Leader. The Leader will rotate for each round."* Read each step on the Math Talk transparency and ask the team to model each step for the class, without actually solving the problem. Stress the fact that students may talk about how to solve the problem in step 3, but they *may not talk* as they use the calculator to actually solve the problem.

3. Math Talk
Allow time for students to complete the Rain Forest Word Problems worksheet. Everyone does not have to write the same answer; the discussion is just to expose students to different problem-solving strategies. After they finish writing, they return their pencils to the cup. When all pencils are back in, the next person becomes the new Leader.

Journal Idea
Have students make up their own math word problems in their journals. Ask them to trade with a partner who tries to solve the problem correctly.

Rain Forest Word Problems

Solve the problems below using a calculator if needed. Write your answer in the blank. Then clearly explain the steps you took to arrive at that answer.

Name _____

1. Imagine that a certain rain forest in Brazil is 100 square miles in size. Suppose that 38% of that rain forest was cut down to make room for a cattle ranch. How many square miles were left?

Answer: _____

Explanation:

_____
_____
_____
_____
_____
_____

2. Suppose that one square mile of rain forest has a population of 12 scarlet macaws. Imagine that 3 of those birds are captured by poachers to sell for pets. What fraction of the birds remained in the rain forest?

Answer: _____

Explanation:

_____
_____
_____
_____
_____
_____

3. Suppose a sloth started moving down from the canopy at 9:45 a.m. She reached the ground at 11:05 a.m. How long did it take her to reach the ground?

Answer: _____

Explanation:

_____
_____
_____
_____
_____
_____

4. Imagine that it takes $25.00 to save one acre of rain forest. If Mrs. Candler's class earned $68.00 through T-shirt sales and $15.00 from other donations, how many whole acres did her class save?

Answer: _____

Explanation:

_____
_____
_____
_____
_____
_____

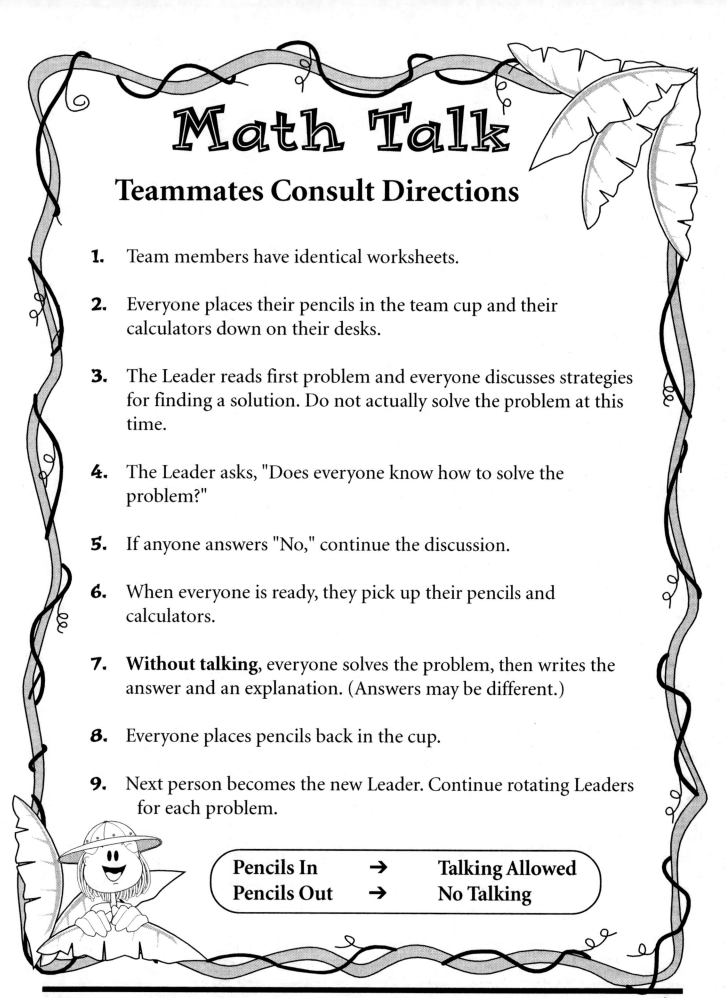

Causes and Effects

In pairs, students list the causes and effects of rain forest destruction. Pairs compare lists and are challenged to add more ideas.

ACTIVITY 30

Steps...

Cooperative Structures
- Pairs Compare
- Stand-N-Share

Content Areas
- Science
- Reading

Materials
- Rain Forest Destruction worksheet (1 per pair)
- Colored pencils (2 different per pair)

Literature Links
Why Save the Rain Forest? or other suitable nonfiction book

Multiple Intelligences
- Verbal/Linguistic
- Logical/Mathematical
- Visual/Spatial
- Naturalist
- Interpersonal

1. Name Problems

Divide each team into pairs. *"What are some of the problems we have studied relating to rain forest destruction? Make a mental list for a few moments."* Pause for at least 30 seconds. *"Now take turns with your partner naming rain forest problems."*

2. Read Aloud

Read aloud Chapter 5 in *Why Save the Rain Forests?* or another nonfiction selection which describes problems associated with rain forest destruction. Ask students to listen for additional rain forest problems they may not have discussed with their partner.

3. List Causes and Effects

Give each pair a Rain Forest Destruction worksheet and two different colored pencils for accountability. *"Some of the problems you heard and discussed are the causes of rain forest destruction. Other problems are the effects of destroying tropical areas. Take turns naming problems. Decide whether the problem is a cause or an effect. List it in the appropriate place on your worksheet. For example, cutting down the rain forest for cattle ranches would be a cause of rain forest destruction so I would list it in the top box. You have 5 minutes to list as many causes and effects as possible."*

4. Pairs Compare

"Now compare your list with your teammates. Take turns calling out items and checking them off. If you don't have something that your teammates mention, add it to your list as they read it aloud. You have 5 minutes to compare lists."

5. Team Challenge

"Pair up with the other pair on your team. As a team, take a few minutes to think of additional rain forest problems you can add to the list. Take turns

Exploring the Rain Forest by Laura Candler • Kagan Publishing • 1 (800) 933-2667 • www.KaganOnline.com

ACTIVITY 30 continued

Causes and Effects

Sample Graphic Organizer

Causes
- drilling for oil
- mining
- clearing land for cattle ranches
- overpopulation

Rain Forest Destruction

Effects
- animals' homes destroyed
- soil erosion
- reduced levels of oxygen

with your partner writing them on your list. Be prepared to share them with the class."

6. Stand and Share

Designate someone to be a Reporter from each team. Ask Reporters to stand with their lists in hand. Call on them to name problems, one at a time, until you have covered the major issues. As each idea is named, have Reporters check it off on their list to avoid duplication. Make sure they have the problems properly classified as a cause or an effect.

Journal Idea

Have students write two paragraphs in their journals, one about the causes of rain forest destruction and the other about its effects.

Causes

Rain Forest Destruction

Effects

The Rain Forest Dilemma

Students develop an understanding of rain forest problems by role playing various people who depend on the rain forest for a living.

ACTIVITY 31

Cooperative Structure
- Jigsaw

Content Areas
- Social Studies
- Reading
- Language Arts

Materials
- Rain Points of View (1 per person)

Literature Links
The Rain Forest Dilemma (1 copy per class)
The Shaman's Apprentice (optional)

Multiple Intelligences
- Verbal/Linguistic
- Naturalist
- Interpersonal

Steps...

1. Read Aloud
If possible, read aloud *The Shaman's Apprentice* by Mark Plotkin and Lynn Cherry. Then read aloud *The Rain Forest Dilemma* to introduce the complexity of the rain forest problem. Students should understand that many developing countries rely on the rain forests to provide food and jobs.

2. Introduce Activity
"Today you will role play different people who depend on the rain forest for a living. Number off in your teams from 1 to 4." Pause. "Each of you will meet in 'expert groups' with others who are playing the same role to discuss these questions: **How do you feel about the rain forest? Should it be protected or should the people who own the land be able to cut down the trees?**"

3. Assign Roles
Write the Rain Forest Roles (see chalkboard illustration) on the board as you assign students to their Jigsaw expert groups. Explain the roles as follows: "Student #1 is a **tribal shaman**, or medicine man who uses rain forest plants to cure illness. Student #2 is a **cattle rancher** who clears rain forests for cattle grazing land. Student #3 is an **ecologist** who studies the importance of the rain forest to living things on earth. Student #4 is a **furniture company owner** who needs tropical hardwood trees to make high quality furniture."

Rain Forest Roles
Expert Group Assignments
- #1 - Tribal Shaman
- #2 - Cattle Rancher
- #3 - Ecologist
- #4 - Furniture Company Owner

4. Form Expert Groups
Give each person one copy of "Rain Forest Points of View." Send each of the four expert groups to separate corners of the room to prepare their position statements. All the

Exploring the Rain Forest by Laura Candler • **Kagan Publishing** • 1 (800) 933-2667 • www.KaganOnline.com

ACTIVITY 31 continued

Points of View

Journal Idea
Now ask students to summarize each person's point of view in their journals. Finally, have them explain their own position on the rain forest dilemma.

cattle ranchers go to one corner, ecologists to another, and so on. Say, *"In your groups, discuss how you feel about the rain forest and whether or not the land owners have the right to cut down trees. List the ideas you heard. After your discussion, write a paragraph describing your position. Back up your position with facts and details. You will return to your original teams to share your statements."*

5. Teams Reunite and Share

After students write their position statements, have them return to their original teams and take turns reading their statements. Make sure they announce their roles before reading their statements.

Variations

- **Paired Reading** – Instead of reading "The Rain Forest Dilemma" aloud, duplicate enough copies for each pair to have one copy to share. Ask partners to take turns reading paragraphs to each other. At the end of the article, have them take turns quizzing each other about what they learned in the article.
- **Read Antonio's Rain Forest** – Instead of (or in addition to) *The Shaman's Apprentice*, read *Antonio's Rain Forest* by Anna Lewington. This book describes the life of a rubber tapper's family and the importance of preserving the rain forest for its inhabitants. You may want to change the role of **shaman** to **rubber tapper** for the Points of View activity.
- **Explore Ethnobotany** – After reading *The Shaman's Apprentice*, have students explore the science of ethnobotany by visiting The Ethnobiology and Conservation Team Web site *(www.ethnobotany.com)*. Then change the role of **ecologist** to **ethnobotanist** for the Points of View activity.

The Rain Forest Dilemma

A Precious Natural Resource

Rain forests cover less than 5% of the Earth's surface, but they are one of the Earth's most precious natural resources. In addition to being beautiful, rain forests provide a home for millions of species of plants and animals. Rain forests are sometimes called the "lungs of the earth" because their trees produce vast amounts of oxygen. Their roots hold the soil in place and prevent erosion. Their leaves release moisture into the air. This moisture affects weather systems around the world.

Rain forests also provide homes for many tribes of natives. Their medicine men, or shamans, have known for centuries that rain forest plants can cure many illnesses. Scientists are beginning to use this information to cure modern diseases. One example is the drug taxol, which comes from the bark of the yew tree. This drug is used to treat cancer patients.

Many everyday products originally came from the rain forest. Sugar and coffee were first discovered in rain forests. Wicker furniture and rubber tires are both rain forest products. Even chocolate comes from a tropical plant, the cacao tree!

Rain Forest Destruction

So why are rain forests being destroyed? To understand the answer, look at a map of rain forest locations on earth. Almost all rain forests are found in developing 3rd world countries. Most people in these countries live in poverty. For centuries, rain forest natives have turned to the forests to supply their needs. They cleared small patches of farmland by cutting and burning the trees, a practice known as slash-and-burn agriculture. They tended their farms until the soil was depleted. Then they cleared another patch of forest. This method worked because only a handful of natives lived in the forest.

But more and more people in these 3rd world countries are leaving over-crowded cities to make their homes on rain forest land. Trees are cut to make room for roads and houses. Rain forest land is being destroyed at a rate of 2 acres each second! That's the size of two U. S. football fields!

Rain forests are also destroyed when large companies buy the land and clear it for economic profit. Rain forest land is cheap, which is why it is often cleared to make room for cattle ranches. Logging companies cut down the trees for hardwood furniture and paper products. Still other companies destroy the rain forest to extract resources deep within the earth. Trees are cut down when companies drill for oil or mine metals such as aluminum. As a result of these practices, more than half of the world's rain forests have already been destroyed.

The Dilemma

Like most problems, the rain forest dilemma has no easy answers. People in rich countries believe that rain forests should be preserved. They believe that rain forests provide oxygen and other resources needed by the entire planet.

Yet many people in poor 3rd world countries disagree. Clearing the land provides jobs and money desperately needed in developing countries. They want to use their land to improve their way of life. They point to rich countries like the United States and say that years ago these countries cleared their own land for profit. They feel that it's unfair for rich countries to ask people in poor countries to stop cutting down trees.

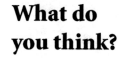

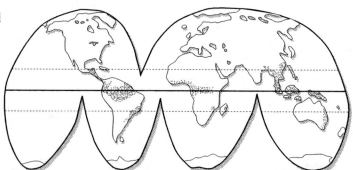

Rain Forest Points of View

Role:_____ Name: _____ #____

Pretend you are the person named above. Think about your answer to the following question:
- How do you feel about the rain forest?
- Should it be protected or should the people who own the land be able to cut down the trees?

Discuss your ideas with your Expert Group and list them below:

Write a paragraph describing your position:
_____
_____
_____
_____
_____
_____
_____
_____
_____
_____

Agreement Circles

The class forms a circle with the teacher in the middle. The teacher reads a statement and students move forward to show their level of agreement.

ACTIVITY 32

Cooperative Structure
- Agreement Circles

Content Areas
- Science
- Social Studies

Materials
- Belief Statements (1 set per class)

Multiple Intelligences
- Verbal/Linguistic
- Visual/Spatial
- Bodily/Kinesthetic
- Naturalist
- Interpersonal
- Intrapersonal

Steps...

1. Form Circle
Take your class to a large open area and have them stand in a circle. Stand in the center of the circle holding the set of Belief Statement cards.

2. Introduce Activity
"There are many different points of view concerning rain forest problems. Today we are going to explore our feelings on some of these issues. I am going to read a statement. If you agree, step forward according to how strongly you agree with the statement. If you strongly agree, take several steps forward and stand close to me. If you disagree, stay where you are. Don't step forward."

3. Agreement Circles
Read each statement and ask students to step forward according to their level of agreement. After everyone moves, the students will be in concentric circles with you in the center. Give students 10-15 seconds to reflect on where their classmates stand on an issue: "Look around; do your classmates agree with your stance or disagree? Have students turn to a partner and discuss their position. Before reading the next statement, have students form the original circle once again.

Journal Idea
After completing several rounds of Agreement Circles, have students write about one or more of their beliefs in their journals. You may want to write the belief statements on the board to help them remember the points that were discussed.

Belief Statements

 Saving the rain forest is the most important environmental issue of this decade.

 Rain forest products are important in my life.

 People should boycott fast food restaurants that use beef raised on cleared rain forest land.

 Rain forest trees should not be cut down for any reason.

 The U.S. Government should give money to rain forest countries to help preserve the tropics.

 Poor countries should not be allowed to cut down their rain forests, even though doing so would improve their economy.

 Laws should be passed banning the use of rain forest hardwood lumber for any reason.

 I would like to visit a rain forest one day.

Save the Rain Forest

Students listen to a story and discuss ways they can help save the rain forest.

ACTIVITY 33

Cooperative Structures
- Pair Discussion
- RoundTable
- Stand-N-Share

Content Areas
- Social Studies
- Science
- Reading
- Language Arts

Materials
- **Kid Power** worksheet (1 per team)
- Internet connection (optional)

Literature Links
Save My Rain Forest by Monika Zak

Multiple Intelligences
- Verbal/Linguistic
- Visual/Spatial
- Naturalist
- Interpersonal
- Intrapersonal

Steps...

1. Pair Discussion
Divide teams into pairs. *"We have studied rain forest problems. What do you think our responsibility is regarding the rain forest? What can we do about these problems?"* Give students 10-15 seconds of think time. *"Now pair with your partner and discuss your ideas."*

2. Read Aloud
Read aloud *Save My Rain Forest.* This is the true story of a boy who walked 870 miles to help save a Mexican rain forest.

3. RoundTable Ideas
Give each team one copy of the Kid Power worksheet. *"What are some things we can do to help the rain forests? Discuss your ideas with your team. Pass the worksheet around the team and take turns adding ideas to the list."* If your students have trouble thinking of ideas, have them visit the Kids Corner of the Rainforest Action Network Web site *(www.ran.org).*

4. Stand and Share
Designate someone on each team to be a Reporter. Ask Reporters to stand with their lists in hand. Call on them to name ideas, one at a time. As each idea is named, have Reporters check it off on their list to avoid duplication. Ask Reporters to sit down when everything is checked off. You may want to have students make a class list to post in the room.

Journal Idea
Ask students to think of things they personally will do to help save the rain forests. In their journals, have them write a short environmental pledge naming the action they plan to take.

Exploring the Rain Forest by Laura Candler • Kagan Publishing • 1 (800) 933-2667 • www.KaganOnline.com

Kid Power

What can kids do to help save the rain forest?

Tropical Tunes

In teams, students create songs to celebrate what they have learned about the rain forest.

ACTIVITY 34

Cooperative Structures
- RoundRobin
- Stand-N-Share
- Team Project

Content Area
- Science
- Social Studies
- Language Arts
- Music

Materials
- Blank transparencies (1 per team)
- Tropical Tune Topics (1 per class)
- Transparency pens (1 per team)

Multiple Intelligences
- Musical/Rhythmic
- Interpersonal

Steps...

1. Introduce Activity

"Today we will celebrate what we have learned about the rain forest by writing songs. Each team will write their song on a different aspect of the rain forest, such as animals, plants, products, or reasons for destruction. At the end of the activity, each team will present their song and teach it to the class."

2. Assign Roles

Number students in teams off from 1 to 4. Assign the following roles by number or let students decide the roles among themselves. The Music Director must be someone who feels comfortable with singing.
- #1 – Recorder
- #2 – Reporter
- #3 – Music Director
- #4 – Song Writer

3. RoundRobin Tunes

"What are some familiar tunes that you think most people can hum or sing easily? Take turns naming songs that you think most people know. I would like the Recorder to list all ideas on a sheet of paper." Allow five minutes for teams to list ideas. If students have trouble thinking of song titles, give a few starter ideas (see below).

Familiar Tunes

Row, Row, Row Your Boat
Twinkle, Twinkle, Little Star
Christmas Carols
Take Me Out to the Ball Game
London Bridge
Three Blind Mice
Mary Had a Little Lamb

Exploring the Rain Forest by Laura Candler • Kagan Publishing • 1 (800) 933-2667 • www.KaganOnline.com

ACTIVITY 34 continued — Write Around

6. Team Project

Allow students time to create a song based on their topic but using a tune of their own choosing. The Music Director is responsible for leading the song and keeping the group "on key." The Song Writer is responsible for writing down the words of the team's rain forest tune. When each team is finished, have the Recorder write the words of the song on a blank transparency. Encourage students to practice the manner in which they will stand before the class and present the song.

7. Team Presentations

Ask each team to present its song to the class. Have them place the words to the song on the overhead projector and present the song for the class one time on their own. Then ask them to sing it again so the class can join in. If possible, arrange for your class to present their Tropical Tunes to another class or as a part of school assembly.

4. Stand-N-Share

Ask all Recorders to stand and share their ideas with the class, one at a time. As they name the tunes, write them on the board. Call on each person to share one idea at a time, and ask the other Recorders to check off each idea as it is read aloud. Ask Recorders to sit down when they have checked off all musical tunes on their list.

5. Assign Topics

Cut apart the Tropical Tune Topics. Ask the Music Director from each team to come forward to select one without looking.

Tropical Tune Topics

Why the Rain Forest Is Important	What Kids Can Do to Help
Animals	Plants
Products	People
Causes of Rain Forest Destruction	Effects of Rain Forest Destruction
Location	Climate

Puppet Shows

Students work in teams to prepare acts for a class rain forest puppet show.

ACTIVITY 35

Cooperative Structures
- Spend-A-Buck
- Team Project

Content Areas
- Science
- Language Arts
- Visual Arts/Drama

Materials
- Rain Forest Bucks (5 per person)
- Puppet show stage or large cardboard box
- Construction paper
- Glue
- Pictures of rain forest plants and animals
- Small paper bags, socks, tongue depressors, and other materials for making puppets
- Tape or CD of rain forest sounds

Multiple Intelligences
- Verbal/Linguistic
- Logical/Mathematical
- Visual/Spatial
- Musical/Rhythmic
- Bodily/Kinesthetic
- Naturalist
- Interpersonal
- Intrapersonal

Steps...

1. Introduce Activity

"Today we will begin to plan and prepare a class puppet show to share what we have learned about the rain forest and its problems. Everyone will help decorate the stage. Then each team will prepare one act for the puppet show."

2. Decorate Stage

Prepare the puppet show stage by cutting a window in a large box. Cover the stage with green construction paper. Distribute materials and ask each person to draw and cut out two plants to decorate the rain forest stage. As they finish each plant, have them come forward and glue it in place.

3. Discuss Team Acts

Ask students to discuss ideas for their team act and write each idea on a separate piece of scrap paper. "Talk about your ideas for your team puppet show act. Use your imagination. You might want to plan a news story, an interview with a rain forest animal, a commercial to save the rain forest, or a story about someone who visits the rain forest. Write each idea on a separate piece of paper."

4. Spend-A-Buck

Give each person 5 paper bucks. "Use your 5 bucks to vote on your favorite ideas. You may only spend 1 buck on your own idea. Place all 5 on your favorite or 1 buck on each of your top choices. Spend your bucks now." When all bucks have been placed on the ideas, say: "Now work together to count the votes for each idea. Decide which idea had the most votes."

5. Choose Roles

"To prepare for the puppet show, you will need to write a script, create homemade puppets, and practice your act. In your teams of four, two students will be Script Writers

Puppet Shows

and two will be Puppet Makers. Take a few minutes now to decide who would like to have each role."

6. Prepare Team Acts

Allow several days for students to write scripts, make puppets, and practice their acts. Let them use the rain forest tape or CD as needed to provide realistic background sounds. If possible, let each team have time to practice with the stage. If one team finishes early, let them decide on the order of the acts and prepare an introduction for the class puppet show.

7. Present Puppet Show

Present the final show to another class if possible.

Rain Forest Bucks

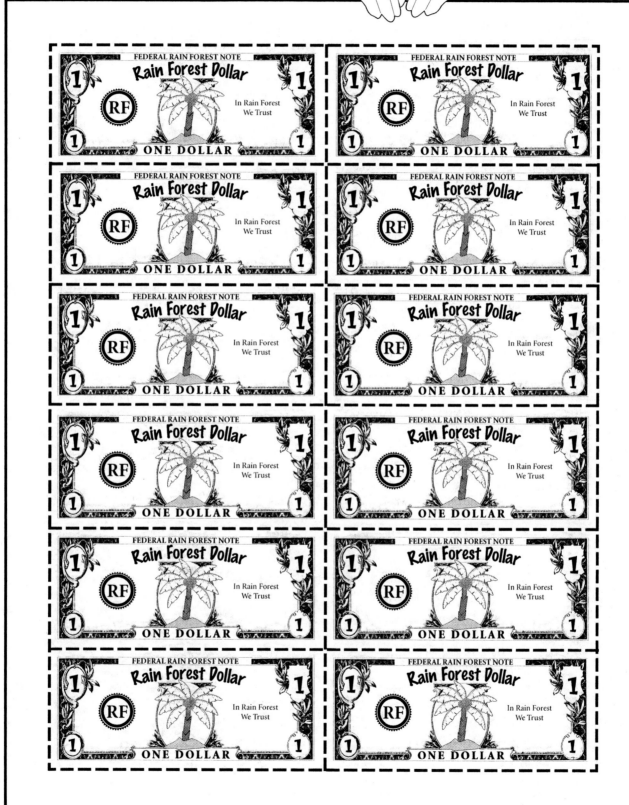

Concept Mapping

Students review rain forest concepts by working in teams to create graphic organizers.

ACTIVITY 36

Cooperative Structures
- Team Project
- RoundTable
- Team Discussion

Content Areas
- Mathematics
- Science
- Social Studies
- Health
- Reading
- Language Arts

Materials
- Poster paper or butcher paper (1 sheet per team)
- Colored pencils, crayons, or markers (1 pack per team)
- **Rain Forest Concepts** worksheet (1 per team)
- Scrap paper

Multiple Intelligences
- **Verbal/Linguistic**
- **Visual/Spatial**
- **Interpersonal**
- **Intrapersonal**

Steps...

1. Introduce Activity
Give each team one copy of the Rain Forests Concepts worksheet. *"As we finish our rain forest unit, we need to review all the ideas we have learned. It's important to see how the different concepts we have learned are actually related in many ways."*

2. RoundTable
"Think back about all the things we have studied, and take turns listing them on the worksheet. Don't bother to use complete sentences... just pass the sheet around and list words and phrases that represent concepts we have studied. Keep listing ideas until you have at least 20 or 30 words and phrases."

3. Team Discussion
"Now look at all your ideas and try to organize them into categories. For example, if someone listed 'iguana' and someone else wrote 'sloth,' the category would be 'animals.' What other important categories can you think of? Talk it over with your team and list your category ideas on a separate sheet of scrap paper."

4. Distribute Materials
Give each team a piece of poster paper or another large sheet of paper. Give them an assortment of colored pencils, markers, or crayons to complete their concept maps.

5. Begin Concept Maps
"Each team is going to create a Team Concept Map of all the ideas learned during this unit. One person begins by drawing a circle in the middle of the poster board. Write the words 'Tropical Rain Forests' inside the circle. Now take turns drawing smaller ovals around the middle to represent the major categories. Fill in each oval with the name of one category. Use lines to connect each small oval to the central idea." Demonstrate on the board.

Exploring the Rain Forest by Laura Candler • Kagan Publishing • 1 (800) 933-2667 • www.KaganOnline.com

ACTIVITY 36 continued

Concept Mapping

6. Add Details

"Now add the words and phrases you listed earlier. Each idea should be connected to its category in a logical manner. As you work, you may decide as a team to change your categories or add new ones. If you see two ideas that go together, draw arrows to connect them. Use your concept map to show everything you have learned and how it all fits together. Take turns writing on the map… everyone must stay involved throughout the activity."

Journal Idea

After students finish their concept maps, post them in the classroom. Have students write a paragraph in their journals summarizing the most important concepts they learned during the unit of study.

Sample Concept Map

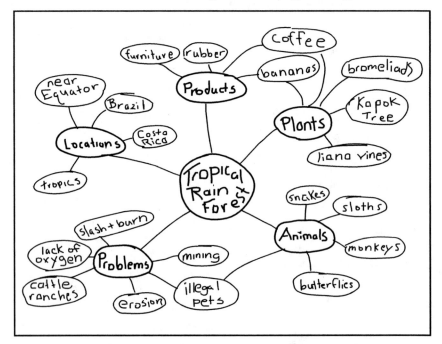

Rain Forest Concepts

Take turns listing the rain forest concepts we studied.

Cooperative Learning Structures

Structure 1

Agreement Circles

1. The class forms a large circle with the teacher in the center.

2. The teacher stands in the middle and states an opinion.

3. Students step toward the teacher according to their level of agreement. Students who completely agree step close to the teacher. Students who disagree remain in place.

4. Students turn to a partner in the circle to discuss their reasons for agreeing or disagreeing.

Structure 2

Blackboard Share

1. Teams perform a cooperative activity.

2. A Reporter from each team writes the team's answer or idea on the blackboard, to share with the entire class.

Cooperative Learning Structures

Structure 3

Find Someone Who

1. Each student is given a Find Someone Who worksheet.

2. Students get out of their seats and find a partner.

3. One partner asks the other student one question on his or her worksheet. The partner answers if he or she knows the answer. The student who asked the question records the answer in his or her own words.

4. The person who answered checks to see if the answer was written correctly and signs the form.

5. Students switch roles for another question.

6. Students mix and pair again with new partners until they complete the worksheet.

Structure 4

Jigsaw

1. Students in base teams of four are assigned separate topics for study.

2. Students with the same topic form "expert groups" to study their assignment.

3. Expert groups return to base teams to present the information they learned.

4. The team or class participates in an activity which requires integrated knowledge of all four study topics.

Cooperative Learning Structures

Structure 5

Mix-Freeze-Group

1. The teacher says "mix!" and students mill around the room.
2. The teacher announces "freeze!" and students stop.
3. The teacher announces a group size by naming a number, clapping a pattern, or asking a question requiring a number answer.
4. Students form groups according to the directions.
5. Students left out move to a "lost and found" area. (Rule: They must be included in a group during the next round.)
6. Students continue to mix, freeze, and group according to teacher directions.

Structure 6

Mix-Freeze-Pair

1. The teacher says "mix!" and students mill around the room.
2. The teacher announces "freeze!" and students stop.
3. The teacher says "pair!" and students find a partner.
4. Pairs are given time to discuss a topic or solve problems.
5. Students mix, freeze, and pair again as prompted by the teacher.

Cooperative Learning Structures

Structure 7

Numbered Heads Together

1. In teams, students number off 1 to 4.
2. The teacher asks a question or states a problem.
3. Students put their heads together to discuss responses.
4. The teacher randomly calls a number.
5. Student with the corresponding number stands to share his or her team's response.

Structure 8

Pairs Compare

1. Students work in pairs to generate a list.
2. Pairs pair up to compare ideas.
3. All four students discuss differences in answers and/or add to their responses.

Cooperative Learning Structures

Structure 9

Pair Discussion

1. Students form pairs (either self-selected or assigned by the teacher).

2. Students turn to their partner and discuss topic.

Structure 10

Pair Project

1. Students form pairs (either self-selected or assigned by the teacher).

2. The teacher describes the project and assigns roles if appropriate.

3. Students work with their partner to complete the project.

Cooperative Learning Structures

Structure 11

Rally Robin

1. The teacher announces a discussion topic with a large number of correct responses.

2. Partners take turns naming responses.

Structure 12

Rally Table

1. The teacher assigns a task or set of problems.

2. Students in pairs take turns completing the task or working the problems.

Cooperative Learning Structures

Structure 13

RoundRobin

1. Teacher asks a question or poses a problem.
2. Team members take turns responding orally.

Structure 14

RoundTable

1. The teacher assigns a task or set of problems.
2. Students in teams take turns completing the assignment.

Cooperative Learning Structures

Structure 15

Same-Different

1. Partners face each other with a barrier between them.

2. Partners are given two variations of the same picture and two recording sheets.

3. Partners take turns describing their picture, attempting to find ways that the pictures are alike and different.

4. Students record all the similarities and differences they can find without looking at each other's pictures.

5. Students remove the barrier and compare pictures with their partner.

Structure 16

Showdown

1. Problem or task cards are stacked face down in the center of the team.

2. The first student becomes the Leader and turns over the top card.

3. Individually, each student works out the first problem and write their answer on a sheet of paper.

4. The Leader says, "Showdown!" and

5. Team members hold up answers. Team members compare and check answers.

6. Students repeat steps, rotating the role of Leader for each round.

Cooperative Learning Structures

Structure 17

Spend-A-Buck

1. Each student is given the same number of paper "bucks" or other tokens to "spend."

2. Students vote for a favorite idea or story by placing their bucks or tokens on the items they choose.

3. Students may spend all their bucks on one item or may spend the bucks any way they choose.

4. Bucks are counted to determine the winning item.

Structure 18

Stand-N-Share

1. Teams complete a cooperative activity.

2. A Reporter from each team stands with a list of the team responses in hand.

3. The teacher calls on each Reporter to name one response.

4. Reporters check off each response on their own list so they won't repeat answers.

5. Reporters sit down when they have checked off all responses.

6. The share session is finished when all Reporters are seated.

Exploring the Rain Forest by Laura Candler • Kagan Publishing • 1 (800) 933-2667 • www.KaganOnline.com

Cooperative Learning Structures

Structure 19

Team Discussion

1. The teacher assigns a discussion topic.

2. Students strive for equal participation as they discuss the topic within their teams.

Structure 20

Team Interview

1. One student on each team stands to be interviewed.

2. Team members take turns asking questions for a designated amount of time.

3. The interviewee may say "pass" if he or she chooses not to answer a question.

4. After time is called, a new person stands to be interviewed.

5. Continue until everyone on the team has been interviewed.

Cooperative Learning Structures

Structure 21

Teammates Consult

1 Everyone places their pencils in the center of the team.

2 Person #1 becomes the first Leader and reads the first question aloud.

3 Everyone discusses the answer.

4 The Leader asks, "Does everyone know what they want to write?"

5 If anyone answers "No," students continue the discussion.

6 When everyone is ready, students pick up pencils and write their own answer **without talking**. Everyone does not have to write the same answer.

7 Students put pencils back in the center of team.

8 The next student becomes the new Leader and reads the second problem. The activity continues until all questions are answered.

Structure 22

Team Project

1 The teacher describes the project and assigns roles if appropriate.

2 Working as a team, students share responsibilities as they complete the project.

Exploring the Rain Forest by Laura Candler • *Kagan Publishing* • 1 (800) 933-2667 • www.KaganOnline.com

Cooperative Learning Structures

Structure 23

Think-Pair-Share

1 The teacher poses question or discussion topic.

2 Ten seconds or more of "think time" is given.

3 Students pair with a partner to discuss responses.

4 The teacher calls on students to share his or her response with the class.

Activity 4 - Answers

Rain Forest Sentences for Practice

1. Have you ever been to a rain forest?
2. If not, you've probably heard of rain forests. Some people call them jungles.
3. My mother and I went to the Amazon rain forest last year.
4. We saw many colorful birds, insects, and flowers.
5. We saw bats, bees, and butterflies darting from flower to flower.
6. Pollinated flowers become fruit that will be eaten by parrots, toucans, insects, bats, and other animals.
7. Air plants grow in the tops of trees. They soak up food and water with their leaves and roots.
8. One type of air plant is called a bromeliad. It looks like the top of a pineapple.
9. We use rain forest products when we eat breakfast, water house plants, or fly in a plane.
10. Corn, rice, and tomatoes were first discovered growing in a tropical rain forest.
11. Tea, coffee, sugar, Brazil nuts, and bananas grew in jungle climates.
12. Ronald said, "One of the best known plants is the rubber tree. Its milky sap is called latex."
13. "How is latex made into rubber?" asked Sally.
14. "I don't know," replied Ronald. "We haven't studied that in science class yet."
15. "Will you try to find out how rubber is made?" asked Sally.
16. Chemicals in leaves, flowers, and seeds are used to make everything from perfumes to chewing gum.
17. Hundreds of people take medicines which contain chemicals from rain forest plants.
18. These plants can kill germs, reduce fever, lower blood pressure, and relax muscles.
19. Scientists will visit the Amazon rain forest in Brazil to learn more about these plants.
20. Our lives would be very different if rain forests were destroyed.

Activity 9 - Answers

Rain Forest Layers
Quick Quiz

1. Which of the layers receives only 3% of the sunlight?
   forest floor
2. Which layer is also called the umbrella layer?
   canopy
3. Where does the harpy eagle make its home?
   emergent layer
4. Which layer contains more plant and animal life than any other?
   canopy
5. Where do leaf cutter ants make their home?
   forest floor
6. What layer is just below the canopy?
   understory
7. Which layer contains trees that may be over 200 feet tall?
   emergent layer
8. In which layer will you find the cacao trees whose pods are used for making chocolate? **Understory**

---

canopy   **understory**
emergent layer   **forest floor**

Activity 23 - Answers

Rain Forest Word Problems
(Level A)

1. Scientists counted 23 new species of butterflies, 8 new bird species, and 16 new mammal species in the rain forest. How many new species is this in all?
47 species

2. If a toucan eats 3 pieces of fruit in one hour, how many pieces can it eat in 6 hours?
18 pieces

3. The temperature in one rain forest was 73° in the morning and 82° by afternoon. How much did the temperature change during this time?
9

4. The same amount of rain fell each day for one week. If 14 inches of rain fell in that week, how many inches fell each day?
2 inches

5. A sloth is 20 feet above ground in a cacao tree. If she climbs down at a speed of 4 feet per minute, how many minutes will it take her to reach the ground?
5 minutes

Activity 23 - Answers

Rain Forest Word Problems
(Level B)

1. Brazil's Amazon Rain Forest is the world's largest, covering about 2 million square miles. By comparison, only 4,000 square miles can be found in Australia. How many more miles of rain forest are in Brazil?
1,996,000 sq. miles

2. Many tropical rain forests receive an average of 25 inches of rain a month. Compare this to San Francisco, which receives only 20 inches *per year*. How much more does the average tropical rain forest receive than San Francisco in one year?
25 inches per month x 12 months = 300 inches per year - 20 inches per year = 280 inches

3. Scientists estimate that deforestation destroys an average of 2 plant or animal species per hour. At this rate, how many species become extinct in one year?
17,520 species

4. Many rain forests are being destroyed to make land for cattle ranches. Over 120 million pounds of beef are imported by the U.S. each year. How many quarter pound hamburgers would that make? If each one sold for $2, how much money would Americans spend on rain forest beef in all?
480 million hamburgers - $960 million

5. A sloth, a monkey, a snake, and a frog were climbing up a kapok tree. They were arranged in a column, with the sloth just above the frog. The snake was not at the bottom, and the frog was between the monkey and the sloth. In what order were the animals on the tree?
snake, sloth, frog, monkey (top to bottom)

Activity 29 - Answers

Rain Forest Word Problems

Solve the problems below using a calculator if needed. Write your answer in the blank. Then clearly explain the steps you took to arrive at that answer.

Name _____

1. Imagine that a certain rain forest in Brazil is 100 square miles in size. Suppose that 38% of that rain forest was cut down to make room for a cattle ranch. How many square miles were left?

   Answer: __62 square miles__

   Explanation:

2. Suppose that one square mile of rain forest has a population of 12 scarlet macaws. Imagine that 3 of those birds are captured by poachers to sell for pets. What fraction of the birds remained in the rain forest?

   Answer: __9/12 or 3/4 of the birds__

   Explanation:

3. Suppose a sloth started moving down from the canopy at 9:45 a.m. She reached the ground at 11:05 a.m. How long did it take her to reach the ground?

   Answer: __1 hour 20 minutes__

   Explanation:

4. Imagine that it takes $25.00 to save one acre of rain forest. If Mrs. Candler's class earned $68.00 through T-shirt sales and $15.00 from other donations, how many whole acres did her class save?

   Answer: __3 whole acres__

   Explanation:

Rain Forest Resources

Books

Cherry, Lynne. **The Great Kapok Tree.** Harcourt, Brace, Jovanovich, 1990.
This is the story of a man who begins to chop down a kapok tree in the rain forest. He tires quickly and falls asleep. In his dreams, the animals of the rain forest plead with him to stop cutting down the trees.

Cherry, Lynne and Plotkin, Mark. **The Shaman's Apprentice: A Tale of the Amazon Rain Forest.** Harcourt Brace & Company, 1998.
Based on true events, this book provides an opportunity for students to appreciate Amazonian culture. Deep in the rain forest, a shaman is the "medicine man" who knows the secret remedies found in forest plants. Young Kamanya dreams of becoming his tribe's next shaman, but his dream becomes endangered when a foreigner arrives who appears to have even stronger medicine that the shaman.

Cobb, Vicki. **This Place Is Wet.** New York, NY: Walker and Company, 1989. An excellent nonfiction book for children. *This book describes the rain forest, its people, and its problems in clear, easy-to-read terms.*

Dorros, Arthur. **Rain Forest Secrets.** New York, NY: Scholastic, Inc., 1990.
This book describes the characteristics, various forms of plant and animal life, and destruction of the world's rain forests.

Dunphy, Madeleine. **Here Is the Tropical Rain Forest.** New York, NY: Hyperion Books for Children, 1994.
Cumulative text presents the animals and plants of the tropical rain forest and their relationship with one another and their environment.

George, Jean Craighead. **One Day in the Tropical Rain Forest.** New York, NY: HarperCollins, 1990.
This is the story of Tepui, a young native living in the rain forest. He attempts to find a new species of butterfly desired by a scientist. If he can do so, a wealthy industrialist will buy the rain forest and save it from destruction.

Gibbons, Gail. ***Nature's Green Umbrella.*** New York, NY. Morrow Junior Books, 1994.
Colorful, clear illustrations and simple text make this nonfiction book a must-have for the classroom.

Lessem, Don. ***Inside the Amazing Amazon.*** New York, NY: Crown Publishers, Inc., 1995.
Each of the 4 layers of the rain forest is shown in huge, fold-out illustrations. This is a perfect book for identifying the plants and animals commonly found in the rain forest.

Lewington, Anna. ***Antonio's Rain Forest.*** East Sussex, England: Wayland Publishers Ltd., 1992.
This is the story of Antonio, whose father taps rubber trees in the Amazon rain forest. The text describes his way of life and the rubber tappers' struggle to protect the rain forest.

Lewis, Scott. ***The Rainforest Book.*** Los Angeles, CA: Living Planet Press, 1990.
Although not designed for children, this book is an excellent resource for teachers. It describes rain forest problems and solutions in great detail. It's also a wonderful source of rain forest trivia.

Yolen, Jane. ***Welcome to the Green House.*** New York, NY: Scholastic, Inc., 1993.
Page by page, the beauty of the rain forest unfolds throughout this book. The text is written in a gently flowing poetic style, and the illustrations are excellent.

Silver, Donald. ***Why Save the Rain Forest?*** New York, NY: Simon & Schuster, 1993.
This is a short chapter book filled with facts and information about the rain forest. It makes an informative text for students. All topics are covered, from plants and animals to problems caused by deforestation.

Wilkes, Angela. ***Jungles.*** London, England: Usborn Publishing, Ltd. 1990.
This book is filled with pictures and captions about life in the rain forest. Each page is a separate topic.

Zak, Monica. ***Save My Rainforest.*** Volcano, CA: Volcano Press, Inc., 1992.
This is the true story of eight-year old Omar Castillo who walks 870 miles to fulfill his dream of visiting a rain forest.

Music

Amazon Days, Amazon Nights. Bernie Kraus, Wild Sanctuary Communications, Inc., 1994 (Available from Northwood Products, 1-800-336-5666)
This audio tape features a "sound sculpture" of the Amazon rain forest. The realistic nature sounds provide a suitable background for rain forest activities.

A Month in the Brazilian Rain Forest. Rykodisc, Salem, MA, 1990.
This CD features sounds of nature blended with relaxing musical compositions.

Nature Whispers: Amazon Rain Forest. Composed by Klaus Black and Tini Bieir. Madacy Entertainment Group, Quebec, Canada. 1996
Rain forest sounds are accompanied by relaxing music in this CD.

Tropical Rain Forest. Unison Music, Nashville, TN, 1995
Tropical sounds are enhanced with Celtic harp and pan flute on this restful and relaxing audio CD.

Organizations

Amazon Conservation Team
www.ethnobotany.org
The Amazon Conservation Team is a nonprofit organization committed to meeting the critical needs and challenges in biodiversity conservation. The organization works with communities in tropical America to understand cultures and the ecosystems in which they live. This Web site offers information about the work of ethnobiologists. You can also find out about a newly released IMAX film entitled 'Amazon' which explores the work of one of the Ethnobiology and Conservation Team's founders, Dr. Mark Plotkin.

Conservation International
2501 M. Street NW, Suite 200
Washington, DC 20037
202-429-5660
www.conservation.org
Conservation International (CI) describes itself as "a field-based, non-profit organization that protects the Earth's biologically richest areas and helps the people who live there improve their quality of life. This site offers facts and information about the rain forest, as well as information about what people can do to help.

Earth Foundation
5151 Mitchelldale, Suite B-11
Houston, TX 77092
800-5MONKEY
www.earthfound.com
The Earth Foundation sponsors an Adopt-An-Acre campaign which has helped save over 100,000 acres of rain forest in recent years. They provide an educational packet of lessons for teachers, along with a video explaining the rain forest problem and describing the project. Call for more information.

Earth's Birthday Project
P. O. Box 1536
Santa Fe, New Mexico 87504-1536
800 – 689-4438
www.earthsbirthday.org
e-mail: earbirpro@aol.com
This project's slogan is "Where environmental education makes learning come to life." Started in 1989, the Earth's

Birthday Project has involved over 2 million children and 200,000 teachers across the United States in a variety of hands-on conservation projects.

National Wildlife Federation
8925 Leesburg Pike
Vienna, VA 22184
703-790-4000
www.nwf.org

The National Wildlife Federation is a nonprofit organization that works to protect wildlife and other natural resources. The group provides educational materials and literature on many topics, including rain forests.

The Nature Conservancy
1815 North Lynn Street
Arlington, VA 22209
703-841-5300
www.tnc.org

The Nature Conservancy is a general conservation group, and their web site provides information about rain forest problems as well as other environmental issues.

Rainforest Action Network
221 Pine Street, Suite 500
San Francisco, CA 94104
415-398-4404
www.ran.org
email: rainforest@ran.org

Provides information about the rain forest and how you can help. Teacher's packet and other information available.

This is a good source of current information about rain forest problems worldwide. Be sure to check out the Kids' Corner.

Rainforest Alliance
65 Bleecker Street
New York, NY 10012
212-677-1900
www.rainforest-alliance.com

This Web site, home of the Rainforest Alliance conservation organization, offers a wealth of information about rain forest problems and solutions. Check out the Kids' Zone and the School House for educational information and activities. You can even find an online coloring book of rain forest birds, with downloadable blacklines for coloring.

The Raintree Group, Inc.
1601 W. Koenig Lane
Austin, Texas 788756
(800) 780-5902
www.rain-tree.com
e-mail: raintree@bga.com

The Raintree Group endeavors to save the rain forest by creating a worldwide market for sustainable rain forest products. This Web site provides excellent information about products of the rain forest. It also provides a comprehensive list of rain forest links.

Rainforest Relief
P.O. Box 150566
Brooklyn, NY 11215
(718) 832-6775
http://host.envirolink.org/rainrelief
email: relief@igc.apc.org

This is a rain forest action site that offers up-to-date information about rain forest problems and gives details about how people can help.

World Wildlife Fund
1250 24th Street, NW
Washington, DC 20037-1175
(202) 293 4800
www.worldwildlife.org
e-mail: wwfus@worldwildlife.org

Known worldwide by its panda logo, World Wildlife Fund (WWF) is dedicated to protecting the world's wildlife and wildlands. The largest privately supported international conservation organization in the world, WWF has sponsored more than 2,000 projects in 116 countries and has more than 1 million members in the U.S. alone.

Internet Links

Amazon.com
www.amazon.com

This Web site is an excellent online book and music store, a wonderful source of rain forest books and music. Simply type "rain forest" into their search engine, and you'll find a wealth of resources on this topic. They offer discounted prices as well as secure online ordering and home delivery.

Amazon Interactive
www.eduweb.com/amazon.html

Explore the geography of the Ecuadorian Amazon through online games and activities.

Amazon Alphabet Activity
http://www.eduplace.com/rdg/gen_act/animal/amazon.html

Provides a lesson plan for completing an Amazon ABC book of animals. You'll even find a list of animals for each letter of the alphabet!

Animals in the Rainforest
http://www.geocities.com/RainForest/5798/ani.html

Students will enjoy visiting this site to learn more about rain forest animals. When they click on small pictures of various animals, they are taken to a page with a larger illustration and a brief description of the animal.

Tropical Treasure Hunt
http://home.att.net/~candlers/tropical.htm

This site offers a simple Internet Treasure Hunt for students, complete with questions, links to web sites, and a brief culminating activity.

Worldclimate
www.worldclimate.com
This Web site allows the user to locate temperature and precipitation statistics for thousands of cities worldwide. It provides a perfect place for students to gather weather statistics for rain forest graphing activities.

Computer Software

Amazon Trail (3rd Edition). The Learning Company (www.learningco.com), 1998.
Students will enjoy this interactive rain forest adventure as they travel with their guide down a virtual river, they experience the sights and sounds of the Amazon Rain Forest.

Rainforest Researchers. Tom Snyder Productions, Inc. (www.teachtsp.com), 1996.
This CD-ROM is a part of Tom Snyder's interactive group software collection. The program is designed to be used with an entire class divided into teams of four who are sharing one class computer. Students assume the roles of ethnobotanist, ecologist, chemist, and taxonomist as they participate in a rain forest adventure. This CD-ROM is a part of a kit which includes 28 student booklets and a teacher's guide.

Kagan

It's All About Engagement!

**Kagan is your source
for active engagement in the classroom.**

Check out Kagan's line of books, smartcards, software, electronics, and hands-on learning resources — all designed to boost engagement in your classroom.

Books

SmartCards

Spinners

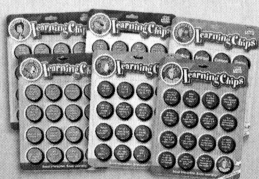
Learning Chips

Posters

Learning Cubes

KAGAN PUBLISHING

www.KaganOnline.com ★ 1(800) 933-2667